EDUCATION REFORMATION

A Teacher's Call for Christian Parents to Abandon the Public Schools and Return to the Word of God

By
Ray Fournier
A Public School Teacher

Education Reformation:
A Teacher's Call for Christian Parents to Abandon the Public Schools and Return to the Word of God

© 2013 by Ray Fournier.
All Rights reserved.

No part of this publication may be reproduced, stored in a retrieval system, or transmitted by any means – electronic, mechanical, photographic (photocopying), recording, or otherwise – without prior permission in writing, unless it's for the furtherance of the gospel and given away free.

Cover design: Joaquin Fernandez president of The Lighthouse, a video production and graphic design firm (www.videoandgraphics.com)
Cover image: 123RF (www.123rf.com)
Page design: Treasure Line Books and Publishing (www.treasurelinebooks.com)

In 6 Days Evangelism
www.EducationReformation.org
E-Mail: In6Days@EducationReformation.org
ISBN-13: 978-0615810911
ISBN-10:n0615810918
Also available in e-Book

Unless otherwise indicated, all scripture quotations are from The Holy Bible, English Standard Version® (ESV®), copyright © 2001 by Crossway, a publishing ministry of Good News Publishers. Used by permission. All rights reserved. Any other Bible versions used will be noted.

PUBLISHED IN THE UNITED STATES OF AMERICA

DEDICATION

I dedicate this book to the glory and honor of my Lord Jesus Christ and to the edification of His bride, the church. In addition, I would like to give special thanks to Lisa, my wife and best friend. Without her love and support this book would have never been possible.

PRIVACY NOTICE

All personal accounts that have been retold in this book are true, but the names have been changed as a courtesy in order to protect the privacy of the individuals involved.

TABLE OF CONTENTS

FOREWORD 1
INTRODUCTION 5
C H A P T E R   O N E: Gospel Centered Motivation 9
C H A P T E R   T W O: The Great Commission, the Sufficiency of Scripture and a Biblical Education 33
C H A P T E R   T H R E E: The 6 Commands and Principles of a Biblical Education 37
    Principle#1: Education belongs to the family supported by the church, not to the state. 37
    Principle#2: Do not be unequally yoked with unbelievers. 41
    Principle#3: Teachers must have a godly character because a student will become like his teacher. 43
    Principle#4: Bad company really does corrupt good character. 47
    Principle#5: A Biblical education is relational. 51
    Principle#6: Biblical Content. 57
C H A P T E R   F O U R: The Education Reformation Manifesto 77
C H A P T E R   F I V E: The Public Schools and the 6 Commands and Principles 83
    Principle#1 84
    Principle#2 87
    Principle#3. 88
    Principle#4 91
    Principle#5 100
    Principle#6 104

CHAPTER SIX: The Public Schools and The Ten Commandments 113
CHAPTER SEVEN: The Public Schools & the Gospel 161
CHAPTER EIGHT: It is Time for Christian Parents to Abandon the Public Schools 165
    Principle#1 166
    Principle#2 166
    Principle#3 167
    Principle#4 167
    Principle#5 168
    Principle#6. 169
CHAPTER NINE: Countering the Salt &Light Argument 175
CHAPTER TEN: Repent 201
CHAPTER ELEVEN: Reform: Applying the Commands and Principles of a Biblical Education 213
    Principle#1 214
    Principle#2 219
    Principle#3 219
    Principle#4 220
    Principle#5 220
    Principle#6 221
CHAPTER TWELVE: Revive 227
Q&A For Parents: Getting Started 229
ABOUT THE AUTHOR 241

FOREWORD

A Manual for a Real EDUCATION REFORMATION
By E. Ray Moore, Th.M.

Education Reformation by Ray Fournier is a worthy addition to a growing body of literature, articles, and books that call pastors, families, local churches and denominations to rescue their children from the secular and humanistic public schools. A clear, comprehensive guide to becoming "more than conquerors," the book calls families to active engagement in Christian education.

Education Reformation systematically presents biblical texts in an easy to find and well-organized manual. Perhaps one aspect that sets *Education Reformation* apart from many other excellent books that promote K-12 Christian education and home-schooling is that Fournier links a Gospel motivation in Chapter 1 and the fulfillment of the Great Commission in Chapter 2 to the biblical mandate for K-12 Christian education or home-schooling. This insight alone makes *Education Reformation* important in the arsenal of books to motivate families and churches to practice K-12 Christian education or home-schooling as part of their walk of faith and obedience. Both chapters are succinct and leave the reader with no ambiguity.

Chapter 3, succinctly organized around six commands and principles for the family, typifies the ease in which the work can be used as a handy instruction manual for study in Sunday school classes, home-schools or home Bible studies.

Many evangelicals who recognize the Great Commission as the primary focus of the New Testament and principal mission of the Church will ascertain through these pages that they have neglected the discipleship of their own children in the family. All too often many of these dear brethren have sent their children into harm's way in the public schools to fulfill the Great Commission or be "salt and light." This tactical error has had tragic consequences for modern evangelicalism. *Education Reformation* addresses this error.

Education Reformation proposes the necessity of parent-directed education and discipleship in the family. Fournier's work should enable Christian families to understand the clash of world views, the harmful influence of the public education system and how to develop practical plans to disciple their children, the next generation, for Christ's Church and kingdom.

As a public school science teacher, Ray Fournier produces accurate, first-hand testimony concerning the harmful impact of public schooling on Christian children. He has woven real-life stories that can alert unsuspecting parents and church leaders to the crisis in the schools through children he knows who have left the Christian faith as a result of their public school experience.

Since graduating with honors from Gettysburg College with a bachelor of science in biology, he has served as a high school science teacher for the last 13 years. Using solid academic credentials in science, he makes the case for creationism in *Education Reformation*. His outspokenness in alerting Christian parents to the dangers in public schools may awaken them to their responsibility to commit themselves whole heartedly to K-12 Christian education or home-schooling.

In Chapter 6, "The Public Schools and the Ten Commandments," Fournier demonstrates how the public school system violates the Ten Commandments and how churches and families contradict their Christian faith when they participate in public schools. The tenor of the book exalts scriptural authority for Christians in all areas of life, especially the education of our children and youth.

Not only has Fournier produced a thoroughly practical and concise book for families and churches, but he may elicit a new generation of books on this crucial topic. He himself represents a new body of leaders entering the battle for the children and for the future of the Church, the family and the culture. If Fournier's instructions are heeded, an "education reformation" could ignite a revival in the land, a biblical reformation, so that once again America could become that "shining city set on a hill" that birthed liberty and the Christian faith throughout this continent and the world.

E. Ray Moore, Chaplain (Lt. Col.) USAR Ret, is founder and president of the Exodus Mandate Project (www.exodusmandate.org). He is veteran of Gulf War I for which he was awarded the Bronze Star.

INTRODUCTION

We need an education reformation!

Out of an average 30 student high school class, 15 are sexually active[1], 23 believe that homosexuality is an acceptable alternative lifestyle[2], 14 don't see a great risk in heavy daily drinking, 12 of them have used marijuana[3], 9 admitted stealing from a store within the past year, 24 admitted to lying to their parents about something significant, 18 admitted to cheating on a test during the last year, and even though they have done these things, 28 out of 30 are satisfied with their personal ethics and character[4].

The moral decline of our youth is truly astounding; but we have an even bigger problem. Between 70%[5] - 88%[6] of children from Christian homes walk away from the visible church by the end of their freshman year in college. That means that more than 7 out of every 10 of our children end up on the road to spiritual destruction

---

[1] Centers for Disease Control and Prevention (CDC)(2009)
[2] Gallup's National Values and Beliefs Survey (2007)
[3] The Partnership at Drugfree.org and MetLife Foundation (2011)
[4] Josephson Institute of Ethics (2010)
[5] LifeWay Research Survey (2007)
[6] Southern Baptist Council on the Family (2002)

instead of being brought up in the discipline and instruction of the Lord and not departing from it.

According to a national survey done by Britt Beemer's America's Research Group, we start to lose our children as early as elementary school, with around 40% of them having decided to walk away from the visible church by the end of middle school. The percentage increases to an alarming 80% by the end of their senior year of high school.[7] The Christian church in America is truly in the middle of a generational crisis.

There are many contributing factors to this crisis, but there is one factor that almost 9 out of 10 Christian families have in common. 89%[8] of Christian parents send their children to the public schools.

At this point, some of you are probably thinking, "What's wrong with the public schools?" The problem is that the public schools teach a secular humanist worldview that is at war with Biblical Christianity.

Secular humanism teaches that humans are the supreme beings of the universe instead of God, and that God either doesn't exist or is simply not necessary. As a result, without God to determine the absolute standard for good and evil, secular humanism teaches that every human being is free to do whatever seems right in his own eyes.

This belief is at the heart of two philosophies that stem from and are taught alongside secular humanism in

---

[7] Britt Beemer's America's Research Group's national survey (2006)
[8] Nehemiah Institute (1988 – 2006) and Britt Beemer's America's Research Group's national survey (2006)

the public schools; post modernism and its close cousin, moral relativism. Post modernism teaches that there is no such thing as absolute truth. While moral relativism teaches that there is no such thing as an absolute standard for good and evil. These philosophies are the exact opposite of what the Bible teaches.

The result of teaching these ungodly philosophies is that the public schools end up indoctrinating 89%[9] of our children for 13 years into a worldview that hates Jesus, discredits the Word of God, sabotages the gospel, and encourages our children to break each and every one of the Ten Commandments. With this being the case, it should be no surprise to learn that after public school indoctrination, less than 1 percent of all Americans between the ages of 18 and 23 have a Biblical worldview[10], including those who came from Christian families. While at the same time, the fastest growing "religious group" in America is made up of people with no religion at all, with 13 million in that group identifying themselves as either atheists or agnostics[11], including many of our own children.

These results clearly point to the reality that the public schools along with the media are succeeding in their efforts to indoctrinate our children into a secular humanist worldview with disastrous effects. Our families are crumbling. Our churches are weakening. And even our nation is now dominated by the same liberal, secular

---

[9] Nehemiah Institute (1988 – 2006) and Britt Beemer's America's Research Group's national survey (2006)
[10] Barna Group's nationwide survey (2009)
[11] Pew Forum on Religion and Public Life survey (October, 2012)

humanist philosophies that are taught in the public schools. "The foundational Biblical concepts that shaped Western nations and cultures are clearly being eroded by the secular education system. Even Abraham Lincoln recognized the dangerous power of schools to shape the next generation: 'The philosophy of the classroom in this generation will be the philosophy of politics, government and life in the next.'"[12]

For more evidence, just look at the last presidential election: government mandated "free" birth control was actually a "political" issue, support for abortion is increasing, homosexual marriage is on the rise (now legal in 10 states), and both Colorado and Washington legalized the recreational use of marijuana. It has become even more obvious that the United States of America is on the road to becoming the next Sodom and Gomorrah. In addition, not only is our culture diving deeper into the depths of human depravity, our government is growing more tyrannical by the day as they continue to erode the freedoms that we take for granted in this country. But no matter how distressing the effects on our society are, the most egregious effect of the public schools' indoctrination of our children is that God is being mocked as the minds and hearts of our children are being stolen by the world, leading millions of them to spiritual destruction. This has to end! It is time to take back the next generation. It is time for an education reformation!

---

[12] Mike Riddle, "Do You Know What Your Children Are Being Taught in School?" Answers Magazine, Vol. 2 No. 3, July – Sept. 2007, p. 51.

CHAPTER ONE:
Gospel Centered Motivation

What would motivate you to sacrifice your precious time, energy, and money to home-school your children or send them to a Christian school dedicated to teaching a Biblical worldview, when you can have the public schools take care of your children's education for "free"? What would motivate you to reform your entire way of life in order to obey God in providing a Biblical education for your children? The motivation of fear? Because if you don't obey, God will punish you? The motivation of reward? Because if you do obey, God will reward you? Neither of these motivations accurately represent God's desire for us. God desires for us to choose to reform our entire way of life because of our love for Him. God desires for us to choose to reform our entire way of life to bring Him honor and glory.

But what would make us abandon our selfish desires, love Him more than ourselves, and want to live for His glory instead of our own? The answer is, His amazing, self-sacrificing love and undeserved kindness that He expressed for us on the cross. Remember, if you are His, it was His love and kindness that led you to repentance and faith in Him (Romans 2: 4). In the same way, by being reminded of the depths of His love for you, you will have more than enough motivation to deny yourself, pick up your cross, and live by His Word; more than enough motivation to rescue your children from the public schools and provide for them a purely Biblical education. In order for us to do this, we need to focus on our primary motivation for every good work; the love of God expressed to us through the gospel of Jesus Christ.

> *"but God shows His love for us in that while we were still sinners, Christ died for us." (Romans 5: 8)*

At this point, some of you might be thinking "Why is the author taking the time to go over the gospel?" "I already know the gospel?" "Why didn't he just go straight to the Biblical principles for education or an exposé on the public schools?" The reason is because the gospel is not just a pre-requisite to the Christian life or even its foundation. The gospel is the Christian life! Trust me. If you don't approach the topic of your children's education with a completely gospel centered focus, you will not only lack the proper motivation to sacrifice what your flesh holds dear in order to follow through on this monumental task, you will ultimately fail to give your children a truly Biblical education.

Now it is time to add fuel to the fire of your passion to live by God's Word through a thorough study of the gospel of Jesus Christ.

The Gospel: Our Primary Motivation

"For God so loved the world, that He gave His only Son, that whoever believes in Him should not perish but have eternal life. For God did not send His Son into the world to condemn the world, but in order that the world might be saved through Him." (John 3: 16 – 17)

This is the most commonly quoted passage about the gospel in America today, but most people have no idea what it means. Most unbelievers don't understand the spectacular nature of the good news of the gospel because they have never been told the bad news that they have sinned against a holy God and justly deserve an eternity in hell. Since they have no idea what they need to be saved from, they don't understand the true value of Jesus' sacrifice on the cross and as a result, they don't understand the love of God. Without this understanding, the gospel's call to repent of their sins and have faith in Jesus as their Lord and Savior is unintelligible.

Even most Christians don't realize just how much they have been forgiven. This has resulted in a lack of passion and love for God, and as a result, a lack of motivation to repent of worldly practices in order to live according to God's Word for His glory. This means that in order to truly understand the gospel, we must begin with the bad news.

Just like a jeweler uses black velvet as a background to maximize the brilliance of the diamonds that he showcases for his clients, the darkness of our sin and the wrath of God that we deserve for our crimes against our Creator make the love of God expressed on the cross shine before our eyes with an unimaginable brilliance.[13] It is this love that leads us to love Jesus more than anything in the universe including more than our own lives and wage war on every sin that put our Jesus on the cross. It is also this love for God that motivates us to disciple our children whom we love to the God whom we love. Our love for God as a result of the gospel is what gives us the passion and determination to glorify God in our educational decisions regardless of any of the inconveniences that an education reformation may bring.

In order to have a greater understanding of the love of God and foster a greater love for God in our hearts that will fuel a greater desire to live by His Word for His glory; I invite you to take a closer look at God's plan of salvation starting at the beginning.

God's Plan of Salvation

In the beginning, God created the universe and declared it to be very good (Genesis 1: 31). There was no sin and as a result, no death, no disease, and no suffering. Compared to the corrupted creation that we experience today, it was the ultimate paradise. On the 6th day of creation, God created Adam and Eve in His image (Genesis1: 26 – 27), sinless and as a result, free to fellowship with God in the Garden of Eden (Genesis 2). If

---

[13] Adapted from Paul Washer's True Gospel Sermon Series

it wasn't for the fall of man, we would have remained sinless and been free to enjoy our fellowship with God in paradise forever.

In the fall of man, Eve was deceived by the serpent (2 Corinthians 11: 3) while Adam rebelled against God by eating the forbidden fruit (Genesis 3), bringing sin and death into the world.

"Therefore, just as sin came into the world through one man, and death through sin, and so death spread to all men because all sinned." (Romans 5: 12)

Adam's sin resulted in the fall of the entire human race from the goodness of God and caused the corruption of all creation (Romans 8: 19 – 22). Adam and Eve being the parents of all who are living (1 Corinthians 15: 22, Acts 17: 26, Genesis 3: 20), passed onto us, their descendants, a corrupted sin nature which makes us slaves to sin (Romans 6: 20 – 21) and spiritually dead (Romans 5: 12, Ephesians 2: 1).

The Apologetics Group, in their documentary "Amazing Grace", describes the human condition after the fall in the following way: "In our fallenness the Bible describes us as:

❖ Darkened in our understanding. (Ephesians 4: 18, 1 Corinthians 2: 14)
❖ Carnally minded, at enmity with God, and incapable of being subject to Him. (Romans 8: 5 – 7)

- ❖ Haters of God and lovers of darkness. (Romans 1: 30, John 3: 19)
- ❖ Dead in our transgressions and sins, by nature children of wrath without the life of God in our souls. (Ephesians 2: 1 – 5)
- ❖ Slaves to our sinful nature, captive to a "my will be done" ethic and epistemology. (Romans 6: 20 – 21, John 8: 34, Titus 3: 3)
- ❖ With hearts that are so twisted with our self-centeredness that out of them come evil thoughts, vulgar deeds, stealing, murder, unfaithfulness in marriage, greed, meanness, deceit, indecency, envy, insults, pride, and foolishness. (Mark 7: 21 – 22)
- ❖ We have all turned; everyone to his own way. (Isaiah 53: 6)
- ❖ Where even the thoughts and imaginations of our hearts are evil continually from our youth. (Genesis 6: 5; 8: 21)"

It's clear from God's Word that because of the fall each and every one of us are born with a totally depraved sin nature that loves sin and hates God. And sadly, because of our sinful natures, we have willfully broken God's commandments (Exodus 20: 1 – 17) countless times.

<u>Commandment #1</u>:
"You shall have no other gods before Me."

And

Commandment #2:
"You shall not make for yourself an idol."

We have worshiped ourselves instead of God by bowing down to the idols of pleasure and self-fulfillment. The truth is, we are selfish by nature and selfishness is idolatry. As a result, it would be impossible for us to count how many times we have broken the first and second commandments.

Commandment #3: "You shall not take the name of the LORD your God in vain."

We have used the name of the LORD our God in vain by using it as a filthy, four-letter word when angry, or without the respect that it's due as a common expression. Blasphemy has become a common figure of speech in our culture as our hearts' natural hatred towards God has escaped our mouths as easily as the air that we breathe.

Commandment#4: "Remember the Sabbath day, to keep it holy."

We have not kept the Sabbath day holy. We thought so little of God that we didn't even set aside a single day to worship Him.

Commandment#5: "Honor your father and your mother."

We have been disobedient to our parents. We thought that God didn't care about the sins of our youth, but we were wrong.

Commandment#6: "You shall not murder."

If we have not murdered in the flesh, we certainly have murdered in our hearts by having even momentary hateful thoughts about people in our lives (1 John 3: 15).

Commandment#7: "You shall not commit adultery."

God sees all sexual activity outside of marriage as sexual immorality. Jesus even said that if you look upon a person to lust after them, you have already committed adultery with them in your heart (Matt. 5: 27 – 28). This means that the breaking of this commandment includes adultery, pre-marital sex, homosexual sex, or even having sexual thoughts about someone who is not your spouse. How many times have we done that?

Commandment#8: "You shall not steal."

How many times have you taken something that wasn't yours? Remember, to God it doesn't matter the item's value or from whom you have taken it from. Theft is theft. If you have stolen even once, God sees you as a thief.

Commandment#9: "You shall not lie."

Have you lost count of how many lies you've told in your life? I sure have.

Commandment #10: "You shall not covet."

Even if you have never stolen a single thing in your life, you have at least been covetous countless times which is idolatry (Colossians 3: 5).

Ultimately, all of us have sinned and fallen short of the glory of God (Romans 3: 23), and we have no idea what that means.

We are like pigs with their slop. Pigs love slop. They gorge themselves on it and wallow in it until every part of their bodies are covered with slop. They don't have any idea how disgusting the slop really is. In the same way, we have no idea how disgusting sin really is. We live every minute of every day immersed in a world that has been corrupted by sin. Sin is something we see, hear, and do almost every moment of our lives. In this life, sin is all around us and in us. We can't escape it. In the end, we have lost all perspective regarding how thoroughly defiling sin really is.

Almighty God, in His perfect holiness, describes sin in different contexts in the following ways:

- ❖ "Dog's Vomit (2 Peter 2: 22)
- ❖ Putrefying sores (Isaiah 1: 5 – 6) NKJV
- ❖ Gangrene (2 Timothy 2: 17)

- ❖ A Dead and Rotting Body (Romans 7: 24) (Matthew 23: 27)
- ❖ And the Stench of an Open Grave (Romans 3: 13)"[14]

God sees us as so completely defiled by our sins that He had the prophet Isaiah compare us to someone with leprosy. As a result, God sees even our good works like a fine white, silk robe placed on a person with the worst kind of leprosy. Moments after touching the puss and rotting flesh, the robe itself becomes defiled.[15] In the same way, our good works are hopelessly defiled by our sins.

> *"We all have become like one who is unclean, all of our righteous acts are like filthy rags. We all shrivel up like a leaf, and like the wind our sins sweep us away"*
> **(Isaiah 64: 6) (NIV).**

In the end, by our own merit, we would all stand guilty before Almighty God and deserve to suffer God's Wrath on evil for eternity in hell.

God Himself has determined that an eternity in hell is the fair and just punishment for rebellion against His Sovereign Rule through the breaking of His Law. Jesus, the very One who loved us so much that He suffered the wrath of God that we deserve for our sins on the cross, spoke about hell more than anyone else in the Bible (Matthew 5: 22, 5:29, 5:30, 8: 11-13, 10:28, 13: 41 – 43, 13: 49 – 50, 18:9, 22: 12 – 14, , 23:15, 23:33, 24: 50 – 51, 25: 30, 25: 46, Mark 9: 43 –

---

[14] List compiled by Todd Friel of Wretched Radio
[15] Adapted from Paul Washer's True Gospel Sermon Series

49, Luke 12: 5, 13: 28, 16: 19 – 41, John 15: 6 etc…).

On the surface this doesn't seem to make sense. How could Jesus' love and the reality of hell go hand in hand? Easy, love hates evil, warns others of imminent danger, and provides a way to be saved from that danger. This is exactly what Jesus did! The following are some of the things that the Word of God says about hell:

Jesus said,

> *"So it will be at the close of the age. The angels will come out and separate the evil from the righteous* (those who have Christ's righteousness as born again believers) *and throw them* (the evil) *into the fiery furnace. In that place there will be weeping and gnashing of teeth. (Matthew 13: 49 – 50) (Explanation added)*

> *"The Son of Man (Jesus) will send His angels, and they will gather out of His kingdom all causes of sin and all law-breakers, and throw them into the fiery furnace. In that place there will be weeping and gnashing of teeth. Then the righteous will shine like the sun in the kingdom of their Father. He who has ears, let him hear." (Matthew 13: 41 – 43)(Explanation added)*

When referring to people who persecute Christians, the Word of God says,

> *"When the Lord Jesus is revealed from heaven with His mighty angels in flaming fire, inflicting vengeance on*

> *those who do not know God and on those who do not obey the gospel of our Lord Jesus. They will suffer the punishment of eternal destruction,"*
> *(2 Thessalonians 1: 7b – 9a)*

The eternal destruction is further described in Revelation 14: 10 – 12:

> *"He also will drink the wine of God's wrath, poured full strength into the cup of His anger, and he will be tormented with fire and sulfur in the presence of the holy angels and in the presence of the Lamb. And the smoke of their torment goes up forever and ever, and they have no rest, day or night," (Revelation 14: 10 – 11b)*

Contrary to those who believe that eternal destruction means that the people who will be thrown into hell are simply going to be annihilated and cease to exist, Jesus was clear that their punishment will go on for all of eternity.

> *"And these will go away into <u>eternal</u> punishment, but the righteous into <u>eternal</u> life."*
> *(Matthew 25:46)(Emphasis added)*

"Eternal punishment ... eternal life. The same Greek word is used in both instances. The punishment of the wicked is as never-ending as the bliss of the righteous. The wicked are not given a second chance, nor are they annihilated. The punishment of the wicked dead is described throughout Scripture as "everlasting fire" (Matthew 5: 41); "unquenchable fire" (Matthew 3: 12); "shame and everlasting contempt" (Daniel 12:2); a place where "their worm does not die, and the fire is not quenched" (Mark 9: 44 – 49); a place of "torments" and "flame" (Luke16: 23, 24); "everlasting destruction" (2Thessalonians: 1: 9); a place of torment with "fire and brimstone" where "the smoke of their torment ascends forever and ever" (Revelation 14: 10,11); and a "lake of fire and brimstone" where the wicked are "tormented day and night forever and ever" (Revelation 20: 10). Here Jesus indicates that the punishment itself is everlasting – not merely the smoke and flames. The wicked are forever subject to the fury and the wrath of God. They consciously suffer shame and contempt and the assaults of an accusing conscience – along with the fiery wrath of an offended deity – for all of eternity. Even hell will acknowledge the perfect justice of God (Psalm 76: 10); those who are there will know that their punishment is just and that they alone are to blame (cf. Deuteronomy 32: 3 – 5)."[16]

If you have not repented of your sins and trusted in Jesus as your Lord and Savior, listen to the warning of your conscience. God declares that all liars, murderers, the sexually immoral, and the unbelieving will have their part in the lake of fire (Revelation 21: 8). No thief, no adulterer, no idolater, and no covetous person will have their part in the Kingdom of God (1 Corinthians 6: 9 – 10).

---

[16] Dr. John MacArthur, The MacArthur Study Bible, p. 1442

The Gospel

Thankfully God is not just holy and perfect in His justice and wrath, God is love.

"God is love. In this the love of God was made manifest among us, that God sent His only Son into the world, so that we might live through Him. In this is love, not that we have loved God but that He loved us and sent His Son to be the propitiation for our sins."
(1 John 4: 8b – 10)

*"Surely He has borne our griefs
and carried our sorrows;
yet we esteemed Him stricken,
smitten by God, and afflicted.
But He was pierced for our transgressions;
He was crushed for our iniquities;
upon Him was the chastisement that brought us peace,
and with His wounds we are healed.
All we like sheep have gone astray;
we have turned—every one—to his own way;
and the LORD has laid on Him
the iniquity of us all."*
(Isaiah 53: 4 – 6)

Jesus Christ, the Creator of the universe, came down from heaven to be born of a virgin, fully God and fully man. He lived a sinless life and satisfied the righteous requirement of the law that you have broken, so that He could take your place on the cross as the perfect sacrifice. On that cross, the Creator died for His creation. On that cross, Jesus suffered the wrath of God that you deserve for your sins, satisfying the justice of God. On that cross, a legal transaction occurred. Your shameful sins were credited to His account and He paid for them in full with His life's blood. At the same time, His perfect righteousness was credited to you so that you could have peace with God. Then on the third day, God the Father raised Him from the dead (Acts 5: 30). On the third day, the Holy Spirit raised Him from the dead (Romans 8: 11). On the third day, He rose Himself from the dead (John 2: 19 – 21, 10: 17 – 18), defeating death and later ascended to Heaven to sit at the right hand of the Father.[17]

Please take a moment to think about the countless times you have broken God's Law including all of your secret sins that would overwhelm you with shame if they were exposed. Now think about the wrath of God that you deserve to suffer in hell for eternity. Realize that you are spiritually dead, incapable of saving yourself, and in your own strength without hope. This is the dark background that magnifies the love of God. The stark contrast between our total depravity, and God's mercy and grace that was expressed on the cross allows us to see the unimaginable brilliance of the love of God, just like the darkness of the night sky allows us to see the brilliance of the stars.[18]

Jesus loves you so much that He took upon Himself

---

[17] Adapted from Paul Washer's "Death Sermon Jam" (www.youtube.com)
[18] Adapted from Paul Washer's True Gospel Sermon Series

all of your shameful sins and suffered God's eternal wrath in your place. If it hasn't already, His infinite love for you should move you to love Jesus more than anything in the universe, even more than your own life, and hate all of your sins that put Him on the cross. Yes you are guilty. Yes you deserve an eternity in hell. But let His infinite kindness lead you to repentance and faith in Him. Throw yourself at His mercy. Confess your sins to Him and apologize for offending Him. Ask Him to forgive you for all of your sins. Turn away from your sins, repent of both your sins and of trusting in your good works. Trust in the work of Jesus Christ alone for your salvation and He will forgive your sins and save you from the eternity in hell that you deserve.

    Salvation is an amazing gift of God. He didn't have to send us a Savior. If He would have decided to send all of us to hell, God would still have been a loving and good God. In the end, justice would have been done and we would only have gotten what we deserve. But thankfully God is love and decided to express His love for us by giving us undeserved mercy and grace. Ephesians 2: 1 – 8 clearly describes our salvation.

> "*<u>You were dead in the trespasses and sins</u> in which you once walked, following the course of this world, following the prince of the power of the air, the spirit that is now at work in the sons of disobedience— among whom we all once lived in the passions of our flesh, carrying out the desires of the body and the mind, and were <u>by nature children of wrath</u>, like the rest of*

> *mankind. But God, being rich in mercy, because of the great love with which He loved us, even when we were dead in our trespasses, made us alive together with Christ— by grace you have been saved— and raised us up with Him and seated us with Him in the heavenly places in Christ Jesus, so that in the coming ages He might show the immeasurable riches of His grace in kindness toward us in Christ Jesus. For by grace you have been saved through faith. And this is not your own doing; it is the gift of God, not a result of works, so that no one may boast." (Ephesians 2: 1 – 8)(Emphasis added)*

Salvation is a purely supernatural act of God. We were spiritually dead, incapable of even calling out to God for help. God alone acts to save sinners. God alone rescues us from our sins and from the eternity in hell that we deserve. It is God's supreme display of His love for us. If He hadn't given us spiritual life, making us born again (regeneration) (Ephesians 2: 4 – 5, John 5:24-25), and drawn us to Christ (John 6: 44), we could not have even believed the gospel (1 Corinthians 1: 18) let alone have saving faith and repent of our sins. It is God's saving work alone and Christ's righteousness alone imputed to us that make us righteous before God. The salvation that God has provided gives us His amazing grace that we do not deserve, and gives God all of the glory.

Sola Scriptura

We learn about this amazing salvation and live our lives by scripture alone.

*"The law of the LORD is perfect,
reviving the soul;
the testimony of the LORD is sure,
making wise the simple;"
(Psalm 19:7)*

*"But as for you, continue in what you have learned and have firmly believed, knowing from whom you learned it and how from childhood you have been acquainted with the sacred writings, <u>which are able to make you wise for salvation through faith in Christ Jesus</u>. All Scripture is breathed out by God and <u>profitable for teaching, for reproof, for correction, and for training in righteousness, that the man of God may be competent, equipped for every good work</u>."
(2 Timothy 3:14-17)(Emphasis added)*

Sola Fide

We are saved through faith alone.

"Therefore, since we have been justified by faith, we have peace with God through our Lord Jesus Christ. Through Him we have also obtained access by faith into

> *this grace in which we stand, and we rejoice in hope of the glory of God."*
> *(Romans 5:1-2)*

Sola Gratia
We are saved by grace alone.

> *"He saved us, not because of works done by us in righteousness, but according to His own mercy, by the washing of regeneration and renewal of the Holy Spirit, whom He poured out on us richly through Jesus Christ our Savior, so that being justified by His grace we might become heirs according to the hope of eternal life."*
> *(Titus 3:5 – 7)*

> *"But the free gift is not like the trespass. For if many died through one man's trespass, much more have the grace of God and the free gift by the grace of that one man Jesus Christ abounded for many."*
> *(Romans 5:15)*

Solo Christo
We are saved in Christ alone.

> *"And there is salvation in no one else, for there is no other name under heaven given among men by which we must be saved." (Acts 4:12)*

"For there is one God, and there is one mediator between God and men, the man Christ Jesus, who gave Himself as a ransom for all, which is the testimony given at the proper time." (1Timothy 2:5-6)

Soli Deo Gloria
We are saved and live for the glory of God alone.

"Sing to the LORD, all the earth!
Tell of His salvation from day to day.
Declare His glory among the nations,
His marvelous works among all the peoples!
For great is the LORD, and greatly to be praised,
and He is to be held in awe above all gods.
For all the gods of the peoples are idols,
but the LORD made the heavens.
Splendor and majesty are before Him;
strength and joy are in His place.
Ascribe to the LORD, O clans of the peoples,
ascribe to the LORD glory and strength!
Ascribe to the LORD the glory due His name;
bring an offering and come before him!
Worship the LORD in the splendor of holiness,
tremble before Him, all the earth;
yes, the world is established; it shall never be moved.
Let the heavens be glad, and let the earth rejoice,
and let them say among the nations, "The LORD reigns!" (1 Chronicles 16:23-31)

> *"Oh, the depth of the riches and wisdom and knowledge of God! How unsearchable are His judgments and how inscrutable His ways!*
> *"For who has known the mind of the Lord, or who has been His counselor?"*
> *'Or who has given a gift to Him that He might be repaid?'*
> *For from Him and through Him and to Him are all things. To Him be glory forever. Amen."*
> *(Romans 11:33-36)*
>
> *"So, whether you eat or drink, or whatever you do, do all to the glory of God."*
> *(1 Corinthians 10: 31)*

This God glorifying salvation is more than enough to show us God's attribute of love, but God does not stop there. He continues to lavish on us gift after undeserved gift. He not only forgives us of our sins and saves us from the just punishment that we deserve; He clothes us with Jesus' righteousness (Romans 5:17) and adopts us as His Children. This makes us heirs of His Kingdom (Galatians 4: 4 – 7) and transforms our relationship where God literally becomes our loving Father and friend. Through Jesus we have become children of God and as a result, we have direct access to the Father in prayer (Hebrews 4: 15 – 16). The intimacy and depth of this loving relationship is seen in the fact that at the point of salvation God indwells us with His Holy Spirit.

> *"Jesus answered him, "If anyone loves Me, he will keep my word, and my Father will love him, and We will come to him and make Our home with him."* (John 14: 23)
>
> *"But when the fullness of time had come, God sent forth His Son, born of woman, born under the law, to redeem those who were under the law, so that we might receive adoption as sons. And because you are sons, God has sent the Spirit of His Son into our hearts, crying, "Abba! Father!" So you are no longer a slave, but a son, and if a son, then an heir through God."* (Galatians 4: 4 – 7)
>
> *"Or do you not know that your body is a temple of the Holy Spirit within you, whom you have from God?"* (1 Corinthians 6: 19a)

God gives us His Holy Spirit to seal us for salvation (Ephesians 1: 13, 4: 30), comfort us with His love and care (Acts 9: 31), enlighten us with His truth (John 14: 26), and to begin the process of sanctification (Titus 3: 5, 1 Corinthians 6: 11). This is the process where God progressively purifies us, day after day taking sins out of our life, leading us to a life of repentance and faith where God progressively transforms us into the image of His Son (Romans 8: 29). During this process, God produces in us the fruits of the Spirit: Love, Joy, Peace, Patience, Kindness, Goodness, Faithfulness, Gentleness, and Self Control (Galatians 5: 22 – 23). And if that wasn't enough, God gives us a new family, countless brothers, sisters, mothers, and fathers united together as His people, His

Church, the body of Christ, united by one Spirit, one Lord, one faith, one baptism, one God and Father of all, who is over all and through all and in all. (Ephesians 4: 4 – 6) Together He has made us into a royal priesthood, a holy nation, a people for His own possession, that we may proclaim the excellencies of Him who called us out of darkness and into His marvelous light (1Peter 2: 9 – 10). Together He has loved us by giving us an eternal purpose in this life, to glorify God in all that we do (1 Corinthians 10: 31) and to fulfill the Great Commission (Matthew 28: 18 – 20).

It was this love that transformed the disciples from the cowards who denied Jesus when the soldiers came to arrest Him, to the fearless apostles who boldly proclaimed the gospel of Jesus Christ until all except one suffered a martyr's death. It is this same love that still enraptures the hearts of men and women today to the point of being willing preach the gospel for the glory of God in countries like Iran and North Korea where to be caught preaching the gospel results in certain death. And if you haven't done so already, it is this same love that should move you to love Jesus more than anything in the universe, including your own life; and to hate and wage war on your sins that put Jesus on the cross. Yes you are guilty and yes you deserve an eternity in hell, but let Jesus' infinite kindness and amazing love lead you to repentance and faith in Him.

It is also this same love of God expressed to us through the gospel of Jesus Christ that humbles us, focuses us on His glory, and fuels the fire of our passion to live by His Word and carry out the Great Commission which includes providing a Biblical education for our children.

CHAPTER TWO:
The Great Commission, the Sufficiency of Scripture and a Biblical Education

The Great Commission is the Primary Purpose of a Christian's Life.

Jesus came to earth to seek and save the lost (Luke 19:10). The primary reason Jesus does not take us up to heaven the moment He saves us is because He wants us to continue in His work. Jesus wants us to seek and save the lost as we strive to fulfill the last command He gave us before He ascended to heaven, the Great Commission.

> *"And Jesus came and said to them, "All authority in heaven and on earth has been given to me. Go therefore and <u>make disciples</u> of all nations, <u>baptizing them</u> in the name of the Father and of the Son and of the Holy Spirit, <u>teaching them</u> <u>to observe all that I have commanded you</u>. And behold, I am with you always, to the end of the age." (Matthew 28: 18 – 20)(Emphasis added)*

What is the Great Commission?

It is clear from the scriptures that the Great Commission not only includes the preaching of the gospel and baptizing new believers, it also includes the making of mature disciples by teaching them to observe all that Jesus has commanded. This is the goal of a truly Biblical education. Ultimately, a Biblical education is the direct application of the Great Commission in our own homes.

Where Should We Start Fulfilling the Great Commission?

Jesus commanded His disciples to be His witnesses in Jerusalem, in all Judea and Samaria, and to the end of the earth (Acts 1: 8). Jesus wanted them to start with local missions and to expand from there to global missions; and this is exactly what the Holy Spirit caused to happen. The question is what does our most local missions' field consist of? The answer is our family. As a result, the Great Commission needs to begin with our family, expand to our friends and extended family, our local community, and then to the rest of the world.

"There are many mission fields, but family presents what may be the greatest untapped evangelistic opportunity before the church today. What is at stake is the salvation of millions of children under the evangelistic and discipleship ministry of fathers and mothers in the home. This is not the only mission field, to be sure, but it is perhaps the most neglected mission field before the church in our time."[19]

What this means for us as parents is that when it comes to the Great Commission our primary responsibility is the evangelism and discipleship of our children.

> *The evangelism and discipleship of our children is one of the most important **good works** God has given us to accomplish.*

One of the reasons God created us in Christ was to accomplish good works for His Glory.

> *"For we are His workmanship, created in Christ Jesus for <u>good works</u>, which God prepared beforehand, that we should walk in them."* (Ephesians 2: 10)
> (Emphasis added)

The evangelism and discipleship of our children, which is at the core of a Biblical education, is one of the most important good works that God has given us to accomplish. Thankfully God has not left us without instructions on how to accomplish this essential good work.

---

[19] Scott Brown, "The Greatest Untapped Evangelistic Opportunity Before the Modern Church", http://www.christianpost.com

The Bible Is All We Need.

God has given us His infallible, authoritative, and sufficient Word to fully equip us for every good work, including how to educate our children.

> *All Scripture is breathed out by God and profitable for teaching, for reproof, for correction, and for training in righteousness, <u>that the man of God may be complete, equipped for every good work.</u>"*
> *(2 Timothy 3: 16 – 17)(Emphasis added)*

Since God has given us everything that we need to be fully equipped for every good work in His Word and the education of our children is one of these good works, we can be certain that God has provided us with specific instructions on how to educate our children. God's Word is all that we need. The reformers' cry of "Sola Scriptura" is at the heart of our education reformation.

The following chapter will examine some of the Biblical commands and principles given to us by God that directly apply to our children's education.

CHAPTER THREE:
The 6 Commands and Principles of a Biblical Education

Jesus said, "If anyone loves me, he will keep my word," (John 14: 23a)

Principle#1: Education belongs to the family supported by the church, not to the state. [20]

"Nowhere in Scripture does a reference exist in which God delegates to the state the authority to educate children."[21] Fathers are the ones that are commanded to train and educate their children. (Ephesians 6: 4, Psalm 78:5-8, and Deuteronomy 6: 1 - 7)

> *"<u>Fathers</u>, do not provoke your children to anger, <u>but bring them up in the discipline and instruction of the Lord.</u>" (Ephesians 6: 4)(Emphasis added)*

---

[20] Exodus Mandate, "Education belongs to the family, supported by the church, and not to the state", July 17, 2012
[21] Exodus Mandate, "Education belongs to the family, supported by the church, and not to the state", July 17, 2012

God Himself has given fathers not mothers, not schools, not churches, and certainly not the state, but fathers this responsibility. As a result, fathers are the ones who will be ultimately held accountable by God for what their children are taught regardless of whether it is taught by the fathers themselves or by the media, peers, churches, and schools that the fathers endorse by sending their children to them for instruction. From God's point of view, fathers by their very position as fathers have been appointed by God as the teachers of their children, and will be held accountable as such by God.

> *"Not many of you should become teachers, my brothers, <u>for you know that we who teach will be judged with greater strictness</u>."*
> *(James 3: 1)(Emphasis added)*

Keep this fact in mind when we later analyze what children are taught in the public schools by their peers and the government curriculum. Whatever the children are taught in the public schools will be laid at the feet of the fathers who sent them there.

> *"And He said to his disciples, "Temptations to sin are sure to come, but <u>woe to the one through whom they come!</u> It would be better for him if a millstone were hung around his neck and he were cast into the sea than that he should cause one of these little ones to sin."*
> *(Luke 17: 1 – 2)(Emphasis added)*

Fathers will also be held accountable by God for the simple fact that they have been ordained by God as the heads of their households. The principle of headship accountability is clearly illustrated in the fall. Just like Adam as the head of his family received 100% of the blame for the fall of mankind even though Eve was the one who was deceived by the serpent and was the first to eat of the forbidden fruit (Romans 5: 12 – 14), in the same way fathers will be held accountable by God for the deception and falling away of their children. They will be charged by God with failing as the heads of their households and stewards of their children's education. This fact is clearly illustrated in the qualifications for pastors/elders in both 1Timothy and Titus.

> *"Now the overseer must be above reproach, the husband of but one wife, temperate, self-controlled, respectable, hospitable, able to teach, not given to drunkenness, not violent but gentle, not quarrelsome, not a lover of money. <u>He must manage his own family well and see that his children obey him with proper respect. (If anyone does not know how to manage his own family, how can he take care of God's church?)</u>"*
> *(1 Timothy 3: 2 – 5) (Emphasis added)*

As you can see, the success or failure of a man's household including his children's obedience (1Timothy 3: 2 – 5) and spiritual well-being (Titus 1: 6) will ultimately be laid at the feet of the father.

Even though God has given fathers the primary responsibility of bringing up their children in the discipline and instruction of the Lord, God has given mothers a vital role in this enterprise. God has given mothers the role of being the fathers' primary helpers in accomplishing the goal a Biblical education (Genesis 2: 18 – 24, Proverbs 1:8, Proverbs 6:20, Song of Solomon 8:2). Since the wife is the only person in the world who is one flesh (Mark 10 7 – 9) with her husband, she is perfectly suited to help her husband fulfill this incredible responsibility. With both father and mother working together as one, parents are more than capable of training their children in the way that they should go so that they will not depart from it (Proverbs 22:6). But if the father is disobedient to God, dead, or otherwise absent, it falls to the mother to accomplish this good work (Acts 16: 1, 2 Timothy 1: 5).

God's Word clearly teaches that the education of children belongs to the family, but God never intended for Christian families to function in isolation. Families separated from the local church are like sheep separated from the flock; easy prey for the predators of this world. Without being part of the flock, these sheep lack the protection, guidance, and encouragement of the flock and its shepherds. With that being said, the church has a very important role to play in the education of our children.

First of all, Jesus, the "Good Shepherd" (John 10: 11 – 16), has charged pastors to take care of His flock (1 Peter 5: 1 – 5). As a result, pastors should be the first ones to sound the alarm concerning the spiritual dangers of public education and to equip fathers and mothers to fulfill their God given ministry to their children

(Ephesians 4: 11 – 16). This training along with the fellowship, accountability, and encouragement that are provided by the body of Christ are essential for our children's education.

Ultimately, if you commit yourselves to being your children's primary source of discipleship, your family will experience the blessings of rich parent-child relationships and the most effective "youth ministry" possible. Having ownership over your children's evangelism and discipleship, which makes up the majority of a Biblical education, is God's prescription for fulfilling His command to train up your children in the discipline and instruction of the Lord.

Principle#2: Do not be unequally yoked with unbelievers.

"<u>Do not be unequally yoked with unbelievers</u>. For what partnership has righteousness with lawlessness? Or what fellowship has light with darkness? What accord has Christ with Belial? Or what portion does a believer share with an unbeliever? What agreement has the <u>temple of God with idols</u>? For we are the temple of the living God; as God said, 'I will make my dwelling among them and walk among them, and I will be their God, and they shall be my people. Therefore go out from their midst, and <u>be separate from them, says the Lord</u>, and touch no unclean thing;

> *then I will welcome you,*
> *and I will be a Father to you,*
> *and you shall be sons and daughters to Me,*
> *says the Lord Almighty.'"*
> *(2 Corinthians 6: 14 – 18)(Emphasis added)*

Most of the time this passage of scripture is applied in the context of a warning to not enter into an unequally yoked marriage, but that is not the only possible application. In the literary context where this verse is found, it is clearly a general principle that is applicable to all aspects of life, with being yoked referring to a close personal partnership. This passage could very well be applied to marriage, business partnerships, close friendships, or any relationship where an unbeliever could apply significant influence on a believer. A partnership with someone in the training and education of our children certainly qualifies as a relationship where an unbeliever could exercise significant influence on a believer's children, family, and ultimately the church. As a result, willingly becoming partners with unbelievers in our God given responsibility to train and educate our children is clearly a violation of this clear Biblical principle. With this being the case, parents need to keep this principle in mind when evaluating the practice of sending our children to the public schools.

Principle#3: Teachers must have a godly character because a student will become like his teacher.

> "He (Jesus) also told them a parable: "Can a blind man lead a blind man? Will they not both fall into a pit? A disciple is not above his teacher, <u>but everyone when he is fully trained will be like his teacher.</u>"
> (Luke 6: 39 – 40)(Explanation and Emphasis added)

As parents, if we choose to have our children taught by someone besides ourselves, we need to make sure that the teacher in question is a born again Christian who is growing in holiness and is committed to teaching a Biblical worldview. The reason for this is because if he is not, our children will suffer harm.

> "Whoever walks with the wise becomes wise, but the companion of fools will suffer harm." (Proverbs 13: 20)

This principle reminds me of what happened to Ricky Sanchez[22]. Ricky reached a crossroad in his life while I was right in the middle of trying to witness to a pro-abortion, pro-homosexual, illegal alien smuggling, socialist, Buda worshipping, "Christian" teacher named Ms. Carson[23]. Ms. Carson was truly a fervent evangelist for her mystical version of the secular humanist faith.

---

[22] Name has been changed.
[23] Name has been changed.

She was relentless in her attempt to turn her students away from Jesus. She even openly encouraged her classes to experiment with homosexuality as part of their "education". In response to her activities, I had several serious conversations with her regarding the gospel and her need to be truly saved, as well as what God thought about her beliefs. Around this time was when Ricky's life began to change.

Ricky had been one of my wife's piano students for several years and had just finished a semester of being in my class. While I was right in the middle of my conversations with Ms. Carson, Ricky was taking Ms. Carson's class and spent his lunch periods socializing with Ms. Carson and many of her young disciples. The result of his time with her was truly heart breaking.

Even though my wife and I had been ministering to him outside of school for a couple of years, Ricky was drawn in by Ms. Carson's defiling ideologies. He went from having a year-long crush on one of the girls in my honor's biology class to experimenting with homosexuality to eventually becoming enslaved in a homosexual relationship.

We found out about this relationship when he showed up unexpectedly in a state of emotional distress. Immediately, my wife gave me a quick call on my cell phone, and within minutes, I was having a heart to heart conversation with Ricky.

In that conversation, Ricky told me everything. He told me how he had finally come to realize that he had been a homosexual from birth even though just a couple of months earlier he had been obsessed with winning the heart of a girl in my class. He went on to tell me how he met his homosexual partner and fell in "love" with him, followed by how he came out of the closet, told his parents, and how he was immediately kicked out of his house by his father.

This was truly a surreal moment. While he was telling me his story, I couldn't help but be astonished by the fact that this conversation was even happening considering the fact that he already knew where we stood on the issue of homosexuality.

Anyway, here was Ricky, homeless, crying his eyes out, and bearing his broken heart to me. All I could do was share the love of Christ with the young man. First, I gave him a hug and reminded him of how much my wife and I loved him. Shortly after I hugged Ricky, he calmed down and listened intently to what I had to say. I shared with him exactly what the Bible said about the sin of homosexuality, followed by a detailed explanation of the gospel. I shared with him about the total depravity of the human heart and how his heart was deceiving him, the utter hopelessness of our situation as slaves to sin, but how Jesus could give him a new heart, cleanse him from his sin, and set him free from all unrighteousness, including the sin of homosexuality.

Throughout the conversation, he asked many questions that I patiently answered by showing him what God said in His Word. The conversation could not have gone better. In the end, I embraced him again, prayed for him, and told him that if he wanted, he could stay at our house until he was able to be reconciled with his parents.

Sadly, Ricky never made it to our home. Instead, he moved in with his homosexual partner, who was older and lived in his own apartment. Ultimately, due to Ms. Carson's influence, Ricky truly suffered harm; and his story is only the tip of the iceberg. Most public school teachers hold many of the same liberal beliefs as Ms. Carson but are more discrete in their attempts to indoctrinate their students.

As parents, we must be very careful when choosing teachers for our children because it is inevitable that *"everyone when he is fully trained will be like his teacher" (Luke 6: 40b).*

If we avoid putting our children under the instruction of Biblical fools who are by their very natures wicked, lovers of sin, and scoffers, and instead choose to evangelize and disciple our children to delight in the law of the LORD and to meditate on it day and night, our children will be blessed.

> *"Blessed is the man*
> *who walks not in the counsel of the wicked,*
> *nor stands in the way of sinners,*
> *nor sits in the seat of scoffers;*
> *but his delight is in the law of the LORD,*
> *and on His law he meditates day and night."*
> *(Psalm 1: 1 – 2)*

Principle#4: Bad company really does corrupt good character.

"Whoever walks with the wise becomes wise, but the companion of fools will suffer harm." (Proverbs 13: 20)

"Do not be deceived: "Bad company ruins good morals." (1 Corinthians 15: 33)

The peers that we allow our children to have indirectly and sometimes directly act as teachers for our children. God made it perfectly clear in His Word that peer pressure <u>will</u> influence our children. Contrary to popular belief, this influence does not have to be in the form of direct instruction or pressure. Children simply watch what other children say and do, and in short order, copy them to one degree or another. The peer culture that they are immersed in inevitably rubs off on them.

Even as adults we are not immune to the influence of the culture around us. For a Biblical example all we have to do is look at the story of Lot and Sodom and Gomorrah (Genesis 18 and 19). This is a story of a righteous man who was greatly distressed and tormented by the wicked deeds that he saw and heard day after day while living in Sodom (2 Peter 2: 6 – 8), but in the end he was so tainted by the sexually perverted culture around him that when placed under pressure, he somehow thought that it was acceptable to offer up his daughters to be raped by the men of Sodom in order to protect his guests (Genesis 19: 4 – 11). In the same way, we as adults in our own modern Sodom and Gomorrah like culture are not free from our culture's influence. Sadly, because we are immersed in this culture, most of the American church does not have any idea how much we have compromised with the world. In many ways we have become like righteous Lot and lost our Biblical perspective in regards to our culture.

The following analogy explains what has happened to us. If a frog were to be tossed into a pot of boiling water, the frog would immediately try to jump out. But if that same frog were to be placed in a pot of room temperature water and then we slowly raised the temperature little by little, the frog would become desensitized and before he could realize it, he would be boiled alive. That is exactly what has happened to us in our own culture. As a result of the consistent incremental corruption of our culture over the last 100 years, just like that frog, we have become too desensitized to notice how tainted we have become by the world's philosophies and practices compared to the pure standard of the Word of God. The American church has not only been compromised by sensuality, a lack of modesty, in the sexual vulnerability of our daughters due to our culture's recreational dating practices, and in our ungodly entertainment choices, it has also been compromised by materialism, feminism, psychology, evolution, moral relativism, and a paralyzing fear of man that has led to a general reluctance to preach the gospel of Jesus Christ. In addition, I sincerely believe that the practice of sending our children to the public schools is just another example of our desensitization.

The curriculum and the student culture of the public schools have consistently gotten worse in such a gradual way, that even though between 70%[24] - 88%[25] of children from Christian homes are walking away from the visible church by the end of their freshman year in college, around 89%[26] of proclaimed Christian parents still have not noticed that the souls of their children are being boiled alive in the black cauldron that is the public schools. Ultimately, if we as adults are that susceptible to being tainted by the culture that we live in, how much more easily are children affected by the peer culture that we place them in?

Children are more easily influenced by their peer culture than adults.

God's Word is clear that children are more spiritually vulnerable than adults. Their hearts are filled with foolishness.

"Foolishness is bound up in the heart of a child;"

---

[24] LifeWay Research Survey (2007)
[25] Southern Baptist Council on the Family (2002)
[26] Nehemiah Institute (1988 – 2006) and Britt Beemer's America's Research Group's national survey (2006)

(Proverbs 22: 15a) (NKJV)

As a result, they are more easily led astray.

Notice the description of the nature of children in Ephesians 4: 14 – 15:

> *"so that we may no longer be children, tossed to and fro by the waves and carried about by every wind of doctrine, by human cunning, by craftiness in deceitful schemes. Rather, speaking the truth in love, we are to grow up in every way into Him who is the head, into Christ," (Ephesians 4: 14 – 15)*

In these verses the nature of new believers is directly compared to the nature of children. Both are characterized by a lack of maturity and wisdom that would lead them to be "tossed to and fro", "carried about by every wind of doctrine", and easily deceived. As much as we as adults can be influenced by our surrounding culture, our children are even more susceptible to being deceived and led astray by false teaching, worldly philosophies, and the sinfulness of their peer culture. This fact should be heavily considered when making educational decisions for our children.

Any idea that our children will be a good influence on a larger group or that children should be used as missionaries in the public schools ignores the Bible's clear teaching on the nature of children and God's declaration that bad company corrupts good character.

Children, by their very natures are spiritually vulnerable and should be protected until they become well equipped born again believers who are no longer children. Ultimately, based on these facts, sending our children into a situation like the public schools where they will try to indoctrinate our children into a God hating, morally relativistic, secular humanist worldview and where they will be immersed in a toxic student culture is a recipe for disaster.

"Do not be deceived: "Bad company ruins good morals."
(1 Corinthians 15: 33)

Principle#5: A Biblical education is relational.

The goal of a Biblical education is the Great Commission; the making of disciples and teaching them to observe everything that Jesus has commanded. This process involves more than just imparting knowledge. It involves the shaping of a person's character through a close personal relationship between the student and his teacher. A strong personal relationship where the teacher takes his student under his wing and shares his life with him is at the core of Biblical discipleship. This is the context where a Biblical education happens. This is what I have come to call the relational principle of education.

On the surface this principle seems like it could be accurately applied in the context of either home-schooling or at a Bible based Christian school that is committed to personal discipleship. But the question is, according to the Bible, who are supposed to be the teachers of children? According to our culture it could be anyone; but as Christians we should not be relying on our culture for our methodology. The only people in the Bible that are directly commanded to teach children are their parents, fathers (Ephesians 6: 4, Psalm 78:5-8, and Deuteronomy 6: 1- 7) and mothers (Proverbs 1:8, Proverbs 6:20, Song of Solomon 8:2). With this being the case, I cannot help but conclude that the home-school setting is the setting where this principle can be most accurately applied.

Keep in mind that I am not saying that a Bible based Christian school would not be a huge improvement over public education. It certainly would! What I am saying is that if you do choose to send your children to a Christian school instead of home-schooling, you would not be choosing the most accurate application of this principle. In addition, you would miss out on the blessing of having even stronger parent-child relationships as well as the opportunity to train the character of your children through the consistent application of Biblical discipline.

In order to fully explore the benefits of the application of this principle, it will be necessary to focus on the setting where parents are the primary teachers of their children. To start our exploration of this principle, the best place to begin is Deuteronomy 6: 5 – 7:

"You shall love the LORD your God with all your heart and with all your soul and with all your might. And these words that I command you today shall be on your

> *heart. <u>You shall teach them diligently to your children, and shall talk of them when you sit in your house, and when you walk by the way, and when you lie down, and when you rise</u>." (Emphasis added)*

Deuteronomy 6: 5 – 7 instructs parents to provide a Biblical education as they live daily life with their children. There doesn't seem to be even a single aspect of life that is excluded; "when you sit in your house", "when you walk by the way", "when you lie down", "when you rise". This all-encompassing educational setting has its challenges but is overflowing with blessings.

In this setting, the parents have complete control over their children's education. We control the content of instruction, the schedule, the student culture/peer influences, and their exposure to the world. In this setting, parents can walk alongside their children as they expose them to the world while simultaneously teaching them how to look at the world and its many issues from a Biblical perspective. In addition, this educational setting is the only one that allows for the consistent training of our children's character by the application of Biblical discipline.

God gave the responsibility of discipline to parents not the state, school, or church (Ephesians 6: 4). Biblical discipline is a very important part of a Biblical education. As a result, I recommend that you contact your pastors and elders to obtain detailed instruction and wisdom on how to lovingly conduct Biblical discipline that is tailor made for the individual qualities of your children.

When parents are this focused on the personal training and education of their children, quantity time becomes quality time to the tenth power. Loving your children by living daily life with them, teaching, guiding, and training them when *"you sit in your house, and when you walk by the way, and when you lie down, and when you rise" (Deuteronomy 6: 7b)* has the greatest potential for fostering the strongest possible parent-child relationships. The bonds of love and care that can be made when the relational principle of education is applied in love are unheard of anywhere else in our American culture. While the rest of the world is trembling with fear as they await what they consider to be the inevitable rebellion of their children during the teenage years, those of us who apply this principle in a gospel centered way, focused on the love and care of our children for the glory of God can be confident that family unity will be preserved with minimal issues as the children transition from childhood to adulthood.

This reminds me of a conversation that I had with a good friend of mine who also happens to be a Christian brother and co-worker with me as teachers in a public high school. In our conversation, my friend expressed great concern about the fact that his 9 year old daughter was only a few years away from becoming a "rebellious teenager". He was having these concerns even though so far, as a homeschooling father, he was not having any problems raising his daughter in the discipline and instruction of the Lord. During this conversation, I reminded him how what seems inevitable following the world's philosophy of education is not inevitable when applying God's philosophy of education to our children.

Every day we work with teenagers who have been raised in the public schools. We see countless examples of varying degrees of teenage rebellion and family dysfunction on a daily basis. But what seems "normal" and "inevitable" at a public high school is not the result that the Bible promises when applying God's philosophy of education.

In the public schools, the media and their peers are the primary influences on children, followed by the government curriculum, and finally their parents. In general they spend 7 hours/day, 180 days/year for 13 years of their life being indoctrinated into a morally relativistic, secular humanist worldview by the public schools. That comes to a total of 35 hours/week, 1260 hours/year; 16,380 hours total for their entire public school education. In addition, part of that time as well as most of the rest of their time each day is spent being corrupted by a toxic peer culture and media that instructs them to love sin and rebel against authority, especially the authority of their parents. No wonder most of the teenagers that we teach on a daily basis don't have close relationships with their parents and usually hold to a completely different worldview than their parents. This is especially true if their parents are conservative Bible believing Christians.

What we see on a daily basis in the public schools is

the complete opposite of the Biblical education model that my friend and I are carrying out with our families. In the Biblical model, the children spend the majority of their time with their parents, and as a result, we are their primary influence, followed by the church, and then their peers and media which we control. The contrast could not be starker. The influences that are listed in the following table are listed from most to least influential.

The Public Schools	**The Biblical Model**
1. Peers and Media	1. Parents
2. Public School Curriculum	2. Church
3. Parents	3. Peers and Media

These two educational models are polar opposites. As such, we should expect the results of each to be as distinct as their differences. Thankfully we are already starting to see the fruit from this Biblical education model in many Christian homeschooling circles. In these circles, families are thriving, parent-child relationships are rich and strong well into adulthood, and teenagers seem to have a maturity well beyond their years. These results are a sharp contrast to the family dysfunction, rebellion, immaturity, and pain that is so often the result of the public education system.

Principle#6: Biblical Content.

One of the cornerstones to a Christian education is strong gospel centered, Biblical content focused on the Great Commission stemming from an unwavering commitment to the infallibility, sufficiency, and authority of Scripture.

The Great Commission

Some churches are seeing a revival in Biblical evangelism. Pastors are equipping their flocks on how to effectively share the gospel and are mobilizing their churches to go out into their communities to fulfill the Great Commission. We all need to praise God that this has come to pass and take part in the preaching of the gospel for the glory of God and the salvation of men. As I said before, I believe that the only reason God doesn't just take us to heaven the moment He saves us is because of the Great Commission. As a result, seeking to fulfill the Great Commission for the glory of God needs to be our life's purpose.

A father needs to begin the process of carrying out the Great Commission in his own household. This involves the daily evangelism and discipleship of his children which includes the educational choices that he makes for them. As a result, the Great Commission needs to be the focus of his children's education.

> *"And Jesus came and said to them, "All authority in heaven and on earth has been given to me. Go therefore and <u>make disciples</u> of all nations, <u>baptizing them</u> in the name of the Father and of the Son and of the Holy Spirit, <u>teaching them</u> to observe all that I have commanded you. And behold, I am with you always, to the end of the age."* (Matthew 28: 18 – 20)(Emphasis added)

A Great Commission centered education must begin with the gospel and followed by the intensive discipleship and instruction of our children with the Word of God to observe all that Jesus has commanded. These are the tools which will allow us to impart a purely Biblical worldview to our children and allow them to develop true Christian character. Everything else is secondary. The following are some essential aspects of a Biblical education that address the necessity of providing our children with Biblical content:

1. THE FEAR OF THE LORD:

> *"The <u>fear of the LORD</u> is the beginning of knowledge; fools despise wisdom and instruction."*
> (Proverbs 1: 7)(Emphasis added)

> *"The <u>fear of the LORD</u> is the beginning of wisdom, and the knowledge of the Holy One is insight."*
> (Proverbs 9: 10)(Emphasis added)

"And now, Israel, what does the LORD your God require of you, but to <u>fear the LORD your God,</u> to walk in all His ways, to love Him, to serve the LORD your God with all your heart and with all your soul, and to keep the commandments and statutes of the LORD," (Deuteronomy 10: 12 – 13a)(Emphasis added)

"Blessed is everyone who <u>fears the LORD,</u> who walks in His ways!" (Psalm 128: 1)(Emphasis added)

"As a father shows compassion to his children, so the LORD shows compassion to those who <u>fear Him</u>." (Psalm 103: 13)(Emphasis added)

"The <u>fear of the LORD</u> is a fountain of life, that one may turn away from the snares of death." (Proverbs 14: 27)(Emphasis added)

" if you seek it (wisdom) like silver and search for it as for hidden treasures, then you will understand the <u>fear of the LORD</u> and find the knowledge of God. For the LORD gives wisdom; from His mouth come knowledge and understanding; He stores up sound wisdom for the upright;

> *He is a shield to those who walk in integrity,*
> *guarding the paths of justice*
> *and watching over the way of His saints.*
> *Then you will understand righteousness and justice*
> *and equity, every good path;*
> *for wisdom will come into your heart,*
> *and knowledge will be pleasant to your soul;*
> *discretion will watch over you,*
> *understanding will guard you,*
> *delivering you from the way of evil,"*
> *(Proverbs 2: 4 – 12)(Emphasis and Explanation added)*

From these passages of scripture it is clear that the fear of the LORD is essential to a Biblical education and essential to being a disciple of Jesus Christ. As a result, it is critical for us to impart to our children the fear of the LORD. But how do we accomplish this?

> *"And they sing the song of Moses, the servant of God, and*
> *the song of the Lamb, saying,*
> <u>*'Great and amazing are your deeds,*</u>
> <u>*O Lord God the Almighty!*</u>
> *Just and true are your ways,*
> *O King of the nations!*
> <u>*Who will not fear, O Lord,*</u>
> <u>*and glorify your name?*</u>
> *For you alone are holy.*
> *All nations will come*
> *and worship you,*

for your righteous acts have been revealed."'
(Revelation 15: 3 – 5)(Emphasis added)

From this passage the answer is clear. We need to teach our children the great and amazing deeds that God has done. As a result, since the fear of the LORD is the beginning of knowledge and wisdom, and the way to impart the fear of the LORD to our children is to teach them of the great and amazing deeds that God has done, we need focus on God's role in every subject in our curriculum. The following are some examples:

Science

The study of God's creation (science) can easily be used to teach about the power, wisdom, brilliance, and amazing artistry of our Creator. The size, complexity, and beauty of the universe from its fine tuned physical laws to the brilliant nanotechnology of a single cell to the incredible beauty of the sky at sunset scream that God not only exists but is omnipotent, omniscient, and beautiful beyond description. His infinite love and care for us is even expressed by His compassionate design of our planet that provides for us everything that we could ever need; protection, food, water, shelter, beauty etc… The characteristics of our planet alone compared to the rest of the planets of our solar system demonstrate how much God loves and cares for us. The creation is a testimony of many of the attributes of God and as a result, imparts a sense of awe and wonderment that teaches us the fear of the LORD.

> *"The heavens declare the glory of God,*
> *and the sky above proclaims His handiwork."*
> *(Psalm 19: 1)*

> *It is He who made the earth by <u>His power</u>,*
> *who established the world by <u>His wisdom</u>,*
> *and by <u>His understanding</u> stretched out the heavens.*
> *(Jeremiah 10: 12)(Emphasis added)*
> *"For by Him (Jesus) all things were created, in heaven and on earth, visible and invisible, whether thrones or dominions or rulers or authorities—all things were created through Him and for Him. And He is before all things, and in Him all things hold together. And He is the head of the body, the church. He is the beginning, the firstborn from the dead, that in everything He might be preeminent. For in Him all the fullness of God was pleased to dwell, and through Him to reconcile to Himself all things, whether on earth or in heaven, making peace by the blood of His cross."*
> *(Colossians 1: 16 – 20) (Explanation added)*

History

The subject of history can be used to impart the fear of the Lord by demonstrating how God is the Sovereign King of the universe. He is in control of every single detail of human history from large worldwide events involving the rise and fall of nations to the smallest events in our daily lives. History can be taught to highlight God's direct providential rule over His creation. This is a lesson that even Babylon's infamous king Nebuchadnezzar learned after he was directly humbled by God Almighty:

> *"At the end of the days I, Nebuchadnezzar, lifted my eyes to heaven, and my reason returned to me, and I blessed the Most High, and praised and honored Him who lives forever, for His dominion is an everlasting dominion, and His kingdom endures from generation to generation; all the inhabitants of the earth are accounted as nothing, and He does according to His will among the host of heaven and among the inhabitants of the earth; and none can stay His hand or say to Him, "What have you done?" At the same time my reason returned to me, and for the glory of my kingdom, my majesty and splendor returned to me. My counselors and my lords sought me, and I was established in my kingdom, and still more greatness was added to me. Now I, Nebuchadnezzar, praise and extol and honor the King of heaven, for all His works are right and His ways are just; and those who walk in pride He is able to humble." (Daniel 4: 34 – 37)*

This is a lesson that we must teach our children!

Math

Even math can be used to teach the fear of the LORD.

His brilliance as the one who established the laws of logic are in full display in this subject.

Ultimately, if we want our children to be blessed, everything that we teach our children needs to be saturated by the fear of the LORD.

2. THE CENTRALITY OF THE WORD OF GOD

Our main goal as Christian parents is to see our children become born again believers who live their lives by the Word of God. All that is necessary to accomplish this is the Bible. The Word of God is not only infallible and authoritative, it is also sufficient to lead our children to salvation and to equip them for every good work.

> *"But as for you, continue in what you have learned and have firmly believed, knowing from whom you learned it and <u>how from childhood you have been acquainted with the sacred writings, which are able to make you wise for salvation through faith in Christ Jesus.</u> All Scripture is breathed out by God and profitable for teaching, for reproof, for correction, and for training in righteousness, <u>that the man of God may be complete, equipped for every good work.</u>"(2 Timothy 3: 14 – 17) (Emphasis added)*

Since scripture is sufficient for the salvation and equipping of our children to live lives that will glorify God, studying the Word of God needs to be at the center of their education.

3. A BIBLICAL WORLDVIEW

Everything that we teach our children must be taught from a Biblical worldview. There is no room for worldly wisdom in a Biblical education.

> *"Let no one deceive himself. If anyone among you seems to be wise in this age, let him become a fool that he may become wise. For <u>the wisdom of this world is foolishness with God</u>. For it is written, "He catches the wise in their own craftiness"; and again, "The LORD knows the thoughts of the wise, that they are futile." (1 Corinthians 3: 18 – 20)(NKJV) (Emphasis added)*
> *"For it is written, "I will destroy the wisdom of the wise, and the discernment of the discerning I will thwart." Where is the one who is wise? Where is the scribe? Where is the debater of this age? <u>Has not God made foolish the wisdom of the world?</u> For since, in the wisdom of God, the world did not know God through wisdom, it pleased God through the folly of what we preach to save those who believe." (1 Corinthians 1: 19 – 21)(Emphasis added)*

> *You adulterous people! Do you not know that friendship with the world is enmity with God? Therefore <u>whoever wishes to be a friend of the world makes himself an enemy of God</u>." (James 4: 4)(Emphasis added))*

> *"<u>And do not be conformed to this world, but be transformed by the renewing of your mind,</u> so that you*

> *may prove what the will of God is, that which is good and acceptable and perfect."*
> *(Romans 12: 2)(Emphasis added)*

> *"O Timothy, guard the deposit entrusted to you. <u>Avoid the irreverent babble and contradictions of what is falsely called "knowledge,"</u> for by professing it some have swerved from the faith. Grace be with you."*
> *(1Timothy 6: 20 – 21)(Emphasis added)*

The prohibition on worldly wisdom includes psychology, evolution, post-modernism, or any other idea, philosophy, or lofty opinion that raises itself up against the knowledge of God. The only exception to this prohibition is for the purpose of teaching our children how to tear down these worldly philosophies using apologetics.

4. APOLOGETICS, THE DEFENSE OF THE FAITH

We are commanded by God to have a defense for the hope that lies within us and to destroy every argument that is contrary to God's Word.

> *"but in your hearts honor Christ the Lord as holy, always being <u>prepared to make a defense</u> to anyone who asks you for a reason for the hope that is in you; yet do it with gentleness and respect,"*

(1Peter 3: 15)(Emphasis added)

"For though we walk in the flesh, we are not waging war according to the flesh. For the weapons of our warfare are not of the flesh but have divine power to destroy strongholds. <u>We destroy arguments and every lofty opinion raised against the knowledge of God, and take every thought captive to obey Christ,</u> being ready to punish every disobedience, when your obedience is complete." (2 Corinthians 10: 3 – 6)(Emphasis added)

By teaching our children how to defend their faith and tear down arguments against it, they will be able to both spiritually protect themselves as they go out into the world as adults and be able to use this knowledge when they share their faith with unbelievers.

I strongly recommend Answers in Genesis as a great resource for apologetics training materials, especially if you have questions about evolution and the age of the Earth. Visiting their website will be a blessing to you and your family: http://www.answersingenesis.org/

5. EVANGELISM TRAINING

Since the main purpose of the Christian life is the Great Commission for the glory of God, teaching our children how to share their faith is essential. To equip our children for this monumental task, the first thing we need to do is to have them study the attributes of God and every aspect of the gospel in an in-depth fashion. This kind of extensive study of God and the gospel is necessary training for every born again Christian since we are the ambassadors of the King of the universe (2 Corinthians 5: 20). We need this intensive training to be able to properly represent the King and deliver His message accurately to the world. This is simply basic training for an ambassador of Christ.

The following are some resources that will be very helpful to you as you train your children for evangelism: *One True God Workbook* (attributes of God), *The Truth about Man Workbook*, and *The Gospel's Power and Message* by Paul Washer, and Ray Comfort's *The Way of the Master Basic Training Course* and *The School of Biblical Evangelism*.

These resources can be found on the following websites:

http://www.heartcrymissionary.com/resources/ebooks
http://www.heritagebooks.org/the-gospels-power-and-message/
http://www.wayofthemaster.com/
http://www.biblicalevangelism.com/

In order for your children to be adequately equipped to share their faith, there remains only one more thing to be done. Fathers, as with every other aspect of Christian life, you need to lead by example. You need to make evangelism an integral part of your family's life through hospitality, witnessing to people while going on errands with your children, and even taking your children with you when you go into your local community to witness. There are obviously several factors that will determine how much your children will be involved in these activities, such as whether or not they are born again Christians, whether they have been adequately trained, and whether they are of an appropriate age as determined by their father. But at the very least, the more your children observe their parents sharing the gospel with others, the more they will understand the importance of the Great Commission.

6. PREPARE OUR CHILDREN TO FULFILL THEIR BIBLICAL ROLES AS ADULTS:

This part of their Biblical education will be critical for the spiritual health of their future families for generations to come. Young men need to be taught to become Biblical husbands and fathers (Ephesians 5: 23 – 6: 4, Colossians 3: 19, 1 Peter 3: 7 – 9, 1 Corinthians 13: 4 – 8a, Deuteronomy 6: 4 – 7, etc…) while young women need to be taught to be Biblical wives and mothers (Genesis 2: 18 – 24, Ephesians 5: 22 – 25, Titus 2: 2 – 5, Proverbs 31 etc….)

Just like most other aspects of the Christian life, children will learn these roles best by being instructed by the Word of God and by observing their parents being faithful to the roles God has given them. As a result, if you're not currently being faithful in these God given roles, examine yourselves, repent of your ungodly ways, and seek God's Word as you strive to become a good example for your children.

7. CHRISTIAN DISCIPLINES:

Teaching and modeling the spiritual disciplines of the Christian faith is very important to the Biblical education of our children. The following are some of the disciplines:

Prayer:

> *"Rejoice always, <u>pray without ceasing</u>, give thanks in all circumstances; for this is the will of God in Christ Jesus for you.*
> *(1 Thessalonians 5: 16 – 18)(Emphasis added)*

Bible Study:

> *"But He answered, "It is written,*
> *"'Man shall not live by bread alone,*
> *but <u>by every word that comes from the mouth of God</u>.'"*
> *(Matthew 4: 4) (Emphasis added)*

Scripture Memorization:

> "How can a young man keep his way pure? <u>By living according to Your word</u>. I seek You with all my heart; do not let me stray from Your commands. <u>I have hidden Your word in my heart that I might not sin against you</u>. Praise be to you, O Lord; teach me Your decrees".
> (Psalm 119: 9 – 12)(Emphasis added)

Christian Service:

> "Show hospitality to one another without grumbling. As each has received a gift, use it to serve one another, as good stewards of God's varied grace: whoever speaks, as one who speaks oracles of God; whoever serves, as one who serves by the strength that God supplies—in order that in everything God may be glorified through Jesus Christ. To Him belong glory and dominion forever and ever. Amen." (1 Peter 4: 9 – 11)

Involvement in a Local Church:

> "And let us consider how to stir up one another to love and good works, <u>not neglecting to meet together</u>, as is the habit of some, <u>but encouraging one another, and all the more as you see the Day drawing near.</u> "
> (Hebrews 10: 24 – 25)(Emphasis added)

This is by no means an exhaustive list, but I think you get the idea.

8. PREPARE OUR CHILDREN TO PROVIDE FOR THEIR FUTURE FAMILIES:

Finally, we get to the part of a Biblical education that the rest of the world sees as primary. Don't get me wrong, this aspect of their education is essential (1Timothy 5: 8). If a man wants to eat, he must work (2 Thessalonians 3: 10). As a result, we must do our very best to help our children develop the necessary skills and knowledge to be able to provide for their future families. The reason I placed this aspect of our children's education last is because God has given us different priorities than the world:

"But seek first the kingdom of God and His righteousness, and all these things will be added to you." (Matthew 6: 33)

The Results of Providing a Biblical Education for our Children

No matter how faithfully we provide a Biblical education for our children, there is nothing that we can do to guarantee their salvation. God is 100% Sovereign and has chosen the elect before the creation of the world (Ephesians 1: 3 – 14). But at the same time, God is also a God that uses prescribed means to accomplish His Sovereign will.

"For 'everyone who calls on the name of the Lord will be

> *saved.' How then will they call on Him in whom they have not believed? And how are they to believe in Him of whom they have never heard? And how are they to hear without someone preaching? And how are they to preach unless they are sent? As it is written, 'How beautiful are the feet of those who preach the good news!'"*
> *(Romans 10: 13 – 15)*

As you can see, God uses our preaching of the gospel as a means to accomplish His Sovereign will regarding the salvation of the elect. In the same way, God also uses His prescribed means for the Biblical education of our children in miraculous ways. That is why even though God does not directly guarantee that if we give our children a Biblical education He will automatically save them, He does encourage us that if we walk in His ways, our work in bringing our children up in the discipline and instruction of the LORD will not be in vain.

> *"Blessed is everyone who fears the LORD, who walks in His ways!*
> *You shall eat the fruit of the labor of your hands; you shall be blessed, and it shall be well with you.*
> *Your wife will be like a fruitful vine within your house;*
> *your children will be like olive shoots around your table.*
> *Behold, thus shall the man be blessed who fears the LORD."*
> *(Psalm 128: 1 – 4)*

> *"Train up a child in the way he should go;*
> *even when he is old he will not depart from it."*
> (Proverbs 22: 6)

How this ultimately works out in the mind of God regarding how His complete Sovereignty and our obedience intersect in the salvation or damnation of our children, I do not know. However, I am certain that I must trust in His ways and walk in them, and be encouraged by His grace filled promises, having faith that God's will be done for His Glory and the good of those who love Him (Romans 8: 28).

In the end, repenting of worldly methods and trusting His ways, seeking to submit every area of our lives to Him is the only thing we can do. God will use His prescribed means to accomplish His Sovereign ends. All we can do is be faithful in using His prescribed means.

To those of you who would argue that what has been said in this section somehow violates the fact that God is 100% Sovereign over the salvation of our children, you have to understand that God in His Sovereign will has commanded us to use His prescribed means. If we don't, we are the ones who are in sin for violating His Sovereign commands. For example, God commands us to preach the gospel as a means for Him to accomplish the salvation of the elect. If we sat back and said "God is Sovereign. As a result, I don't have to preach the gospel to the lost." We would clearly be in sin. In the same way, if we said, "God is Sovereign. As a result, I don't have to bring up my children in the discipline and instruction of the LORD. If God wants to save them, He'll save them." we would be equally in sin. The only God honoring option we have is to obey God by using His Sovereignly determined means for the salvation of our children and leave the results up to our merciful and loving God. Either way, God promises to bless our children if we truly give them a purely Biblical education.

> *"Blessed is the man*
> *who walks not in the counsel of the wicked,*
> *nor stands in the way of sinners,*
> *nor sits in the seat of scoffers;*
> *but his delight is in the law of the LORD,*
> *and on His law he meditates day and night.*
> *He is like a tree*
> *planted by streams of water*
> *that yields its fruit in its season,*
> *and its leaf does not wither.*
> *In all that he does, he prospers."* (Psalm 1: 1 – 3)

The following chapter contains a summary of all the commands and principles that we have covered which I believe make up a Biblical education. I have called the Chapter, "The Education Reformation Manifesto". Please read "The Education Reformation Manifesto" carefully while examining the scriptures and engaging in constant prayer. If He hasn't already, I pray that God renews your mind and leads you to join the education reformation.

CHAPTER FOUR:
The Education Reformation Manifesto

We believe that providing a Biblical education for our children is a direct application of the Great Commission and we are motivated by the gospel to provide it for the glory of God.

> *"And Jesus came and said to them, "All authority in heaven and on earth has been given to Me. Go therefore and <u>make disciples</u> of all nations, <u>baptizing them</u> in the name of the Father and of the Son and of the Holy Spirit, <u>teaching them</u> to observe all that I have commanded you. And behold, I am with you always, to the end of the age." (Matthew 28: 18 – 20)(Emphasis added)*

The Great Commission not only includes the preaching of the gospel and baptizing new believers, it also includes making mature disciples by teaching them to observe all that Jesus has commanded. This is the goal of a truly Biblical education.

We believe that the Great Commission begins in our households, expands to our friends and family, our local community, and then to the rest of the world (Acts 1: 8). A Parents' primary responsibility regarding the Great Commission is the evangelism and discipleship of their children.

We believe that one of the reasons God created us in Christ was to accomplish good works for His Glory (Ephesians 2: 10). The evangelism and discipleship of our children, which is at the core of a Biblical education, is one of the most important good works that God has commanded us to accomplish.

We believe that God has given us His infallible, authoritative, and sufficient Word to fully equip us for every good work, including how to educate our children.

> *All Scripture is breathed out by God and profitable for teaching, for reproof, for correction, and for training in righteousness, <u>that the man of God may be complete, equipped for every good work.</u>"*
> *(2 Timothy 3: 16 – 17)(Emphasis added)*

Since God has given us everything that we need to be fully equipped for every good work and the education of our children is one of these good works, we can be certain that God has provided us with specific instructions on how to educate our children. The following are some of the Biblical commands and principles given to us by God that directly apply to the education of our children:

We believe education belongs to the family supported by the church, not to the state. [27]

Fathers are the ones that are commanded to train and educate their children. (Ephesians 6: 4, Psalm 78:5-8, and Deuteronomy 6: 1 - 7)

> "<u>Fathers</u>, do not provoke your children to anger, <u>but bring them up in the discipline and instruction of the Lord.</u>" (Ephesians 6: 4)(Emphasis added)

God Himself has given fathers not mothers, not schools, not churches and certainly not the state, but fathers this responsibility. As a result, fathers are the ones who will be ultimately held accountable by God for what their children are taught.

God has given mothers the role of being the fathers' primary helpers in accomplishing the goal of a Biblical education (Genesis 2: 18 – 24, Proverbs 1:8, Proverbs 6:20, Song of Solomon 8:2). But if fathers are disobedient to God, dead, or otherwise absent, it falls to mothers to accomplish this good work (Acts 16: 1, 2 Timothy 1: 5).

God never intended for Christian families to function in isolation. Families separated from the local church are like sheep separated from the flock; easy prey for the

---

[27] Exodus Mandate, "Education belongs to the family, supported by the church, and not to the state", July 17, 2012

predators of this world. The protection, training, fellowship, accountability, and encouragement that are provided by the body of Christ are essential for our children's education.

We believe that we are not to be unequally yoked with unbelievers in the education of our children.

> "*Do not be unequally yoked with unbelievers. For what partnership has righteousness with lawlessness? Or what fellowship has light with darkness? What accord has Christ with Belial? Or what portion does a believer share with an unbeliever? What agreement has the temple of God with idols?*"
> *(2 Corinthians 6: 14 – 16a)(Emphasis added)*

As a result, willingly becoming partners with unbelievers in our God given responsibility to train and educate our children is a violation of this clear Biblical principle.

We believe teachers must have a godly character because a student will become like his teacher.

> "*He (Jesus) also told them a parable: "Can a blind man lead a blind man? Will they not both fall into a pit? A disciple is not above his teacher, but everyone when he is fully trained will be like his teacher.*"
> *(Luke 6: 39 – 40) (Explanation added)*

We believe bad company really does corrupt good character.

"Whoever walks with the wise becomes wise, but the companion of fools will suffer harm." (Proverbs 13: 20)

"Do not be deceived: "Bad company ruins good morals." (1 Corinthians 15: 33)

As a result, carefully selecting the student culture that our children will be influenced by is of utmost importance.

We believe that a Biblical education involves strong, character building, personal relationships between a student and his teachers. Since God has ordained parents as a child's primary teachers, strong parent-child relationships based on living life together and daily discipleship are essential.

"You shall love the LORD your God with all your heart and with all your soul and with all your might. And these words that I command you today shall be on your heart. <u>You shall teach them diligently to your children, and shall talk of them when you sit in your house, and when you walk by the way, and when you lie down, and when you rise.</u>" (Deuteronomy 6: 5 – 7) (Emphasis added)

We believe that the content of a Biblical education must be Gospel centered (Romans 1: 16) and saturated with the fear of the LORD (Proverbs 1: 7, Proverbs 9: 10), focused on the centrality of the Word of God (2 Timothy 3: 14 – 17), impart a purely Biblical worldview (1Timothy 6: 20, 1 Corinthians 3: 18 – 20, Romans 12: 2), and instruct students in apologetics (1 Peter 3: 15, 2 Corinthians 10: 3 – 6), evangelism (Ephesians 4: 11 – 16), Biblical family roles (Ephesians 5: 23 – 6: 4), prayer (1 Thessalonians 5: 16 – 18), Bible study (Matthew 4: 4), scripture memorization (Psalm 119: 9 – 12), Christian service (1 Peter 4: 9 – 11), involvement in a local church (Hebrews 10: 24 – 25), and career training (1Timothy 5: 8, 2 Thessalonians 3: 10).

If you agree with the Education Reformation Manifesto, please go to the following website to become a signer of the manifesto:
http://www.educationreformation.org/

CHAPTER FIVE:
The Public Schools and the 6 Commands and Principles

In the previous chapters, we established a Biblical standard for our children's education by examining 6 Biblical commands and principles given to us by God that directly apply to our children's education. Now we will evaluate the practice of sending children from Christian homes to the public schools by the Biblical standard.

Before we start this evaluation, I need to remind you that I have worked as a public high school teacher for more than a decade. As a result, many of the details that I am going to share with you regarding the public schools are not just a product of doing the research. I have been an eyewitness to many of these details. Now let's put on our Biblical glasses and look at the practice of sending our children to the public schools through the lens of the Word of God.

Principle#1: Education belongs to the family supported by the church, not to the state. [28]

According to God, fathers have been given the primary responsibility to educate their children, with mothers as their primary helpers, and with the support of the church. Fathers are supposed have complete control over what their children are taught. The question is can a father obey this principle while sending his children to the public schools? The answer is, no. The Government determines what the children will be taught, not the father. In addition, contrary to popular belief, the father doesn't even have the legal right to have his children opted out of subject matter that he finds objectionable. His parental rights stop at the schoolhouse door.

"In 2001, the Palmdale School District in California decided to give a survey to students in its elementary schools. Included in this psychological survey were a number of sex-related questions. These included inquiries into touching one's private parts and thinking about doing so with others, among other fairly explicit questions.

Parents were outraged that this survey was conducted without a proper disclosure to the parents. But the court's decision did not rest upon the district's previous superficial disclosure to parents.

The Ninth Circuit held:

Although the parents are legitimately concerned with the subject of sexuality, there is no constitutional reason

---

[28] Exodus Mandate, "Education belongs to the family, supported by the church, and not to the state", July 17, 2012

to distinguish that concern from any of the countless moral, religious, or philosophical objections that parents might have to other decisions of the School District—whether those objections regard information concerning guns, violence, the military, gay marriage, racial equality, slavery, the dissection of animals, or the teaching of scientifically-validated theories of the origins of life. Schools cannot be expected to accommodate the personal, moral or religious concerns of every parent. Such an obligation would not only contravene the educational mission of the public schools, but also would be impossible to satisfy.

<u>The court went on to make it entirely explicit that once children are left at the public school's front door, all parental control over the child's education ceases.</u>

<u>"In sum, we affirm that the *Meyer-Pierce* right (the right to control their children's upbringing and education) does not extend beyond the threshold of the school door.</u> The parents' asserted right "to control the upbringing of their children by introducing them to matters of and relating to sex in accordance with their personal and religious values and beliefs," by which they mean the right to limit what public schools or other state actors may tell their children regarding sexual matters, is not encompassed within the Meyer-Pierce right to control their children's upbringing and education.

The First Circuit Court of Appeals made a similar outlandish ruling in *Brown v. Hot, Sexy and Safer Productions, Inc.* (1995). This case involved a mandatory, school-wide assembly that contained offensive and suggestive sexual material. The First Circuit said that while parents have the right to choose alternative forms of schooling, they have no constitutional right to direct their child's education inside the public school. Consider how broadly the First Circuit characterized these rights... What the First Circuit said was this: Parents cannot be told by the state to stop teaching their children, but parents cannot stop the state from teaching those children just because the parents do not like what is being taught. None of the cases just described were decided with a balancing test. Every case held that parents' rights had not been burdened or implicated at all. In fact, according to the courts, parents' rights to control the education of their children completely stop at the schoolhouse door." [29]

These court rulings make it perfectly clear that a father cannot obey Principle#1while sending his children to the public schools. In the end, for a father to send his children to the public schools, would be like Esau selling his birthright for a bowl of stew. The father would be giving up his God given authority as a father over his children and his children themselves, for the convenience of a "free" government education.

Ultimately, we must remember that "Christians begin with the belief that children belong to the Lord and are a stewardship to the parents, not the state. Psalm 127:1 says, "Behold, children are a gift of the Lord."

---

[29] Michael P. Farris, J.D., A Dangerous Path, Has America Abandoned Parental Rights?, *reprinted from* The Home School Court Report *(vol. XXII, no. 4)*

There are numerous texts to support this belief, such as Deuteronomy 6:1-9, Proverbs 22:6 and Ephesians 6:1-4. Nowhere in Scripture does a reference exist in which God delegates to the state the authority to educate children. Education belongs to the family, supported by the church, and not to the state"[30]

Principle#2: Do not be unequally yoked with unbelievers.

Public schools are not Christian schools. They do not teach about Almighty God, the fear of the LORD, the Gospel of Jesus Christ, or the inerrancy, sufficiency, and authority of Scripture. Needless to say, they do not hold to a Biblical Worldview. The public schools are temples of secular humanism that specialize in indoctrinating our children into a secular humanist worldview. Sending our children to the public schools clearly yokes us with unbelievers (the public school system itself and many of its teachers) in one of the most important ministries that God has given us, bringing up our children in the discipline and instruction of the LORD. The practice of sending our children to the public schools is a clear violation of this Biblical principle.

Most of us would never set foot into a church that taught heresy, yet we are willing to send our children to sit at the feet of heretics to learn their lies? You need to understand that sending your children to the public

---

[30] Exodus Mandate, "Education belongs to the family, supported by the church, and not to the state",
July 17, 2012

schools to be indoctrinated into secular humanism is equivalent to sending your children to Muslim schools to be indoctrinated into Islamic theology.

> *"What partnership has righteousness with lawlessness? Or what fellowship has light with darkness? What accord has Christ with Belial? Or what portion does a believer share with an unbeliever? What agreement has the temple of God with idols?*
> *(2 Corinthians 6: 14b – 16a)*

Principle#3: Teachers must have a godly character because a student will become like his teacher.

The majority of public school teachers enter the teaching profession for the altruistic purpose of molding the minds of the next generation. Believe it or not, most are truly in the business of education for the sake of the children. The majority are sincere in their good intentions. In fact, I even like many of my colleagues, including my current principal, and desire to see all of them saved. The problem is that according to the Bible, their degrees, likability, and good intentions don't qualify them to teach children, let alone children from Christian homes. Just like in the rest of the world, most public school teachers are not born again Christians who are growing in holiness and committed to teaching a Biblical worldview. Most of them are totally depraved sinners, who are slaves to their sin (Romans 6: 20) just like we all were before salvation, and according to the

Bible are considered Biblical fools. They are the wicked, sinners, and scoffers that we are warned to avoid in Psalm 1. As lost people, by definition, they are lovers of sin and haters of God (Romans 1: 29 – 31, 3: 9 – 20); and sadly, they usually succeed in their goal of molding the minds of the next generation by indoctrinating them into the secular humanist worldview. That is why less than 1 percent of all Americans between the ages of 18 and 23 have a Biblical worldview[31]. As Jesus said, *"everyone when he is fully trained will be like his teacher." (Luke 6: 40)*

In addition, most Christian teachers in the public schools are functionally no better. Most Christian teachers completely hide their Christianity for fear of persecution. Even if a teacher somehow lets their students know that they are a Christian, the teacher is prevented from teaching a Biblical worldview. If they were to openly teach a Biblical worldview or share the gospel with their students, the school administration would have just cause to fire them according to the government's interpretation of the establishment clause. Christian teachers who commit this offense have been and will continue to be fired on these grounds. As a result, in most cases, if a Christian teacher remains in the public schools, by definition, he is most likely not teaching a Biblical worldview.

You see, as soon as the administration finds out that a teacher is attempting to teach a Biblical worldview or share the gospel with his students, he will usually be

---

[31] Barna Group's nationwide survey (2009)

fired in short order. I have come close to being fired for doing this very thing. I have been teaching in the public schools for more than a decade and it is only by God's grace that I have not been fired.

As a missionary in the public schools, I have had to completely change my missionary strategy after my principal made it clear that if I was caught sharing the gospel with a student one more time, I would be fired. Now all of my witnessing encounters with students or former students occur outside of school while I am running errands around town or while street witnessing and open air preaching during town events. The only thing I can do in school is to tear down some secular humanist strongholds and make personal connections. I thank God that my position as a public school teacher has resulted in countless witnessing conversations outside of school.

While I believe it is possible for a Christian to teach in the public schools without sinning, I can tell you from personal experience that it is very difficult. Unless a person is willing to lose their job for the glory of God when they are instructed to sin, I would not recommend entering this missions' field.

Regardless of my missionary activities, as a Christian public school teacher I can do very little to safe guard your children from the doctrines of demons that are taught in the public schools. In addition, within the walls of my school it is impossible for me to help Christian parents bring up their children in the discipline and instruction of the LORD. In the end, here's my message to parents: Do not use Christian teachers like myself as an excuse to send your children to the public schools. Do not send your children to me for instruction. Within these walls, they will not be taught the fear of the LORD which is the beginning of wisdom. As a result, they will not be taught a Biblical worldview.

Principle#4: Bad company really does corrupt good character.

> *"Foolishness is bound up in the heart of a child;"*
> *(Proverbs 22: 15a)* (NKJV)

> *"Whoever walks with the wise becomes wise, but the companion of fools will suffer harm."* (Proverbs 13: 20)

> *"Do not be deceived: "Bad company ruins good morals."*
> *(1 Corinthians 15: 33)*

The Bible couldn't be clearer! Children, by their very natures, are almost guaranteed to be corrupted by an ungodly student culture. And an ungodly student culture is exactly what is found in the public schools.

If I were to tell you the details of the countless stories that I have been told by students regarding the total depravity of the student culture in the public schools and how early these things start happening, you would become physically ill.

We are truly in an era of unprotected daughters, who

are sexually used and abused by their peers; an era where sons have been trained by our culture to become sexual predators that are only interested in their own pleasure.

According to data from the Centers for Disease Control and Prevention (CDC), nearly half (49%) of all 12th grade students, reported being sexually active (that is, they have had sex in the past three months)[32]. Fornication with several partners throughout high school has become the norm. For example, my wife and I have ministered to a girl who had 5 different sexual partners by the time she was 12 and is now a teenage mother. After teaching for more than a decade in a public high school, I can assure you that this is not an uncommon story. I have seen this story play out in front of my eyes time and time again. Some keep their babies and become single mothers while others go through the horror of an abortion.

In our modern American culture, women have gone from being protected and cared for by men, as the Bible teaches, to merely being objects of lust, to be used as sexual playthings. Besides co-ed universities, nowhere is this sociological shift more apparent than in the public schools. Fathers routinely send their daughters to the public schools in outfits, that sixty years ago, only prostitutes would have worn. Pornography conditioned teenage boys feast on these unprotected daughters with their eyes throughout the school day. Later, when those same fathers allow their daughters to go out on

---

[32] Centers for Disease Control and Prevention (CDC), 2009

unsupervised dates with these same boys, their purity is defiled. When the teenage boy gets tired of her and starts to crave a new sexual plaything, the girl gets passed along from one guy to another throughout her high school career. If you add to this the rising acceptance of homosexual lifestyles throughout the student culture, I feel like righteous Lot working in Sodom and Gomorrah, with one exception. After what I have observed, I would never hand my daughter over to this student culture to be violated.

In addition to sexual perversion, drug and alcohol abuse is extremely common and socially accepted by the public school student culture. According to a national study released on April 6, 2011 by The Partnership at Drugfree.org and MetLife Foundation: "Almost half of teens (45 percent) reported they do not see a "great risk" in heavy daily drinking. Only 31 percent of teens strongly disapprove of teens and peers their age getting drunk. And a majority of teens (73 percent) report having friends who drink alcohol at least once a week." In addition, "according to the three-year trend confirmed in the 2010 PATS data, there was a significant 67 percent increase in the number of teens who reported using Ecstasy in the past year (from 6 percent in 2008 to 10 percent in 2010). Similarly, in the past 3 years, marijuana use among teens increased by a disturbing 22 percent (from 32 percent in 2008 to 39 percent in 2010)."

Sexual perversion and drug and alcohol abuse are just the tip of the iceberg when it comes to the fruits that naturally come from the pleasure seeking, rebellious, secular humanist worldview that public school children are being indoctrinated with. The mainstream media and the public schools have stolen the minds of these children. Public school children spend almost every waking hour being brain washed by movies, TV, music, video games, and the public school curriculum. To make matters worse, the public school student culture itself not only reinforces this worldview, but also enforces obedience to it through peer pressure. In the end, these influences result in a public school student culture that I can personally testify is accurately described in Romans 1: 28 – 32:

> *"And since they did not see fit to acknowledge God, God gave them up to a debased mind to do what ought not to be done. They were filled with all manner of unrighteousness, evil, covetousness, malice. They are full of envy, murder, strife, deceit, maliciousness. They are gossips, slanderers, haters of God, insolent, haughty, boastful, inventors of evil, disobedient to parents, foolish, faithless, heartless, ruthless. Though they know God's righteous decree that those who practice such things deserve to die, they not only do them but give approval to those who practice them."*
> *(Romans 1: 28 – 32)*

If you send your children to the public schools, people with these character traits will be your children's friends and primary influences. Do not be deceived, God's Word is true:

> *"Whoever walks with the wise becomes wise, but the companion of fools will suffer harm."* (Proverbs 13: 20)
>
> *"Do not be deceived: "Bad company ruins good morals."* (1 Corinthians 15: 33)

It is important to be aware of the fact that this warning is not just for children from marginally "Christian" households who go to the worst public schools. This warning holds true even for children from doctrinally sound, Bible teaching churches that go to the "best" public schools.

A real life example of this is the story of my former student Ashley Jackson.[33] Ashley was a young lady who took my class as a senior in high school early in my teaching career. She was the daughter of a local pastor from a doctrinally sound, Bible believing church; and her end was truly a tragic one.

One day, while in my class, I overheard Ashley talking to her friends in a very enthusiastic way about praising Jesus at church. She even started singing one of her favorite hymns in a joyous and beautiful tone. I couldn't help but listen and rejoice in my heart at the beautiful words and the heart-felt passion that was emanating from this beautiful young lady. Only a few minutes later, the topic of the conversation shifted, and she started to retell of her adventures during spring break. What came out of her mouth was truly foul. Out of

---

[33] Name has been changed.

the same mouth that praised Jesus in such a beautiful way just minutes earlier came the vilest and most corrupt details about her sexual experiences with several young men during spring break. As the filth of her actions washed over me, I became physically ill. My soul was so vexed that I couldn't help but ask her to step outside of my classroom so I could confront her.

I confronted her regarding the utter hypocrisy of her words and actions, and how she was dragging the name of Christ through the mud, causing the world to blaspheme His Name. I strongly encouraged her to repent of her sins and to throw herself at Christ's mercy. In response, she just stood there quietly, waiting to be allowed back into the classroom. After a few moments of silence, I opened the door and we returned to class.

I didn't see any results from our conversation until the year was about to come to an end. Ashley needed to pass my class in order to graduate, but she was failing. She had a 40% average before taking the final exam. This is when our conversation resurfaced.

Ashley asked another teacher to try to convince me to allow her to pass my class regardless of her average. Trying to be helpful, the teacher came to me and asked me if there was anything I could do. I told her that I would not make any decision concerning her grade until she took the final exam. When her test results were determined a few days later, it turned out that Ashley scored a 39%. In the end, her final average was a 40% which is an F. There was no way she could pass on her own merit, but this did not stop Ashley. She believed that she had the right to pass my class even though she had a failing grade.

    This time, Ashley herself approached me and tried to blackmail me into changing her grade. She told me that if I did not change her grade, she would tell an administrator that I had a religious conversation with her earlier in the year. In response to her threat, I told her that I would not blaspheme my God by lying about her grade. When she heard this, she immediately went to an administrator.

    The next thing I knew, I was called to the office. The administrator immediately brought up the religious conversation, but surprisingly, in short order, the conversation shifted to Ashley's grade. "From what I hear, your wife is about to give birth to your first child. This would not be a good time for you to lose your job. If you value your job and your family, you will change Ashley's grade so she can graduate."

    After hearing this, I was very confused. How did not changing Ashley's grade become the offense? But in the end, I was bound by the Word of God. I could not lie. I told the administrator how it would be a sin for me to lie about Ashley's grade and that there was no way that I could do it because I feared God more than man. At this point in our conversation I thought my job was over, but God had other plans. Surprisingly, the administrator left me alone and found another teacher that was willing to change her grade. Then on the last day of school, Ashley was transferred to the other teacher's class. In the end, on graduation day, I looked on as Ashley walked across the stage. Even though Ashley failed my class, she ended up graduating with honors from "Satan's preparatory academy".

It is obvious that even though she was a pastor's daughter that was brought up in the church, the public school's student culture contributed greatly to her corruption. God's Word is true. Bad company truly does corrupt good morals.

Another example of the truth of these verses was the story of a pastor's family from another doctrinally sound church in our area. During my years of teaching, I had the privilege of teaching 2 out of his 3 children. As a result, I became quite familiar with their family. My wife and I even had the opportunity to personally minister to his middle daughter during a moment of crisis in her life.

Heather Parker[34] came to our home in deep emotional anguish. As she poured out her heart concerning all of the circumstances in her current crisis as well as her entire background and personal experience, it became perfectly clear to both my wife and I what had happened to her family. Even though all three of the children were raised in a doctrinally sound church and were heavily involved in the church's ministries, the public school student culture as well as the public school curriculum brought disaster to her family. Heather was horribly scarred by the couple of years that she spent participating in the public schools' party culture where promiscuous sex and drug use reign supreme. Heather's

---

[34] Name has been changed.

older sister, Karen[35], became a lesbian. Even Heather's younger brother, Matthew[36], who on the surface seemed like a success story, did not escape the public schools unscathed. He was in all honors classes where he achieved a high grade point average and he had an outwardly clean social life, but he too was corrupted by the secular humanist worldview that dominates the public schools. As time went on, he began to doubt the inerrancy and sufficiency of scripture, and eventually abandoned these convictions completely. Now, the Bible is only an add-on to his secular humanist world view. In the end, these true stories are simply a reminder that real life is totally consistent with what the Bible teaches.

"Whoever walks with the wise becomes wise, but the companion of fools will suffer harm." (Proverbs 13: 20)

"Do not be deceived: "Bad company ruins good morals." (1 Corinthians 15: 33)

These true stories that I have shared with you are not the exceptions, they are becoming more and more the norm every year. In addition, not all corruption and sin is obvious and out in plain sight. Many of the children sent to the public schools hide their corruption deep within, trying to pretend that they are who their parents want them to be, only to change their outfits, their

---

[35] Name has been changed.
[36] Name has been changed.

personality, and their moral values as soon as they get to school.

Principle#5: A Biblical education is relational.[37]

God established the relational principle of education to bless families with the greatest opportunity for family unity through the kind of strong personal relationships that can only be established while living life together.

On the other hand, the public schools, based on the philosophies that serve as their foundation, are designed to accomplish the opposite. They are designed to separate the children from their parents and to functionally replace the parents with the state. This is the only way to indoctrinate the next generation into a socialist, secular humanist worldview.

On the surface, many people find this claim to be preposterous, but it is not. All we have to do is to take a closer look at the life and work of the man who was the inspiration for the American public education system in order for us to see the situation more clearly.

The man who inspired our public education system had five children that he never knew. As soon as they were born, one by one, he immediately took them away from their mother and delivered them to the steps of an orphanage, never to see them again. He didn't even take the time to find out whether he had sons or daughters. Do these actions sound like the actions of a man in his right mind? Absolutely not! Yet French philosopher, Jean

---

[37] This section was inspired by Kevin Swanson of Generations with Vision

Education Reformation

Jacques Rousseau was the inspiration for our public education system.

"Fifteen years after abandoning his first child, Rousseau began writing on the subject over which he would have the most profound influence of all – education. His famous book, *Emile*, published in 1762, was entirely devoted to the subject of educating a child. In his book *Rousseau and Revolution* famous historian Will Durant summarized Rousseau's view of education that was expressed in *Emile*: 'Rousseau wanted a system of public instruction by the state. He prescribed many years with an unmarried tutor, <u>who would withdraw the child as much as possible from parents and relatives</u>.'

According to the Encyclopedia Americana (1958 edition), Rousseau's work was precedent setting. 'Highly debatable though these propositions [in Emile] are, they have had immense influence on educational theory, including the 'progressive education' formulated by John Dewey"[38], the father of the American public education system and signer of Karl Marx's Communist Manifesto. This fact makes Jean Jacques Rousseau the grandfather of the American public education system. A system deliberately designed to replace the parents with the state, which is why Karl Marx included <u>free education for all children in public schools</u> as the tenth plank of his Communist Manifesto.

In his Communist Manifesto, Karl Marx describes the ten steps necessary to destroy a free enterprise system

---

[38] Kevin Swanson, "Reversing Rousseau", http://generationswithvision.com

and replace it with a system of unlimited government power in order to transform a country into a communist socialist state. It makes perfect sense that Karl Marx would include public education as one of his ten steps. A government forced, controlled, and tax funded school that separates parents from their children is the perfect place to indoctrinate the next generation into a completely different worldview than their parents, and as a result, control the future of a country.

Stalin effectively applied Marx's ideas when he succeeded in transforming Russia into the communist socialist state formally known as the Union of Soviet Socialist Republics (U.S.S.R.). "Joseph Stalin knew the power of education as a propaganda tool. In just one generation, he converted hordes of the deeply religious Russian people into followers of atheistic Marxism. He said, 'Education is a weapon, the effect of which is determined by the hands which wield it.'[39]"[40]

The sad truth is that just like in the Soviet Union, the modern American public education system was developed by another follower of Karl Marx. John Dewey and his disciples deliberately designed the American public schools to separate children from their parents in order to subject them to secular humanist indoctrination. The only difference is that in the United States it has been done in a more gradual way over the last century. "The

---

[39] Joseph Stalin, interview with H.G. Wells, "Marxism Versus Liberalism," July 23, 1934, Marxists Internet Archive, http://www.marxists.org/reference/archive/stalin/works/1934/07/23.htm
[40] Ken Ham, "Gone In Only One Generation", Answers Magazine, Vol. 8 No. 1, Jan. – Mar. 2013, p. 47.

consequences in America were again confirmed in October 2012, when the Pew Forum on Religion and Public Life released new survey results. The CNN website reported, 'The fastest growing 'religious' group in America is made up of people with no religion at all, according to a Pew survey showing that one in five Americans is not affiliated with any religion.... The survey found that the ranks of the unaffiliated are growing even faster among younger Americans. Thirty-three million Americans now have no religious affiliation, with 13 million in that group identifying as either atheist or agnostic, according to the new survey'[41]."[42] It is no wonder that the United States of America is starting to look more and more like the second coming of the U.S.S.R. But even though we could go on a long tangent regarding the cultural and political implications for our country, I am choosing to approach this issue from a spiritual point of view.

> *"For we do not wrestle against flesh and blood, but against the rulers, against the authorities, against the cosmic powers over this present darkness, against the spiritual forces of evil in the heavenly places."*
> *(Ephesians 6: 12)*

---

[41] Dan Merica, "Survey: One in Five Americans Has No Religion," CNN Belief Blog, http://religion.blogs.cnn.com/2012/10/09/survey-one-in-five-americans-is-religously-unaffiliated/comment-page-3/
[42] Ken Ham, "Gone In Only One Generation", Answers Magazine, Vol. 8 No. 1, Jan. – Mar. 2013, p. 47.

Regardless of the political implications, the real battle is behind the scenes. Satan has used and continues to use the public schools as one of his main weapons in his quest to destroy our children, our families, and as a result, our churches from the inside out. He has deceived most of the American church into sending their children away as soon as possible to daycare centers and then to pre-schools and then to the state controlled K – 12 system. The result of this practice has been obvious for some time now. Our families have been divided, and our now isolated children have become easy prey for ravenous wolves.

Principle#6: Biblical Content.

A Biblical education by definition must provide a child with a Biblical worldview. This is definitely something that you will never find in a public school. Even when there is the rare, state certified Bible course taught in a public school, the Bible is taught as just another book of literature, written by fallible human beings, and valuable only for some of its literary and historical content. It is not taught as the inerrant, sufficient, and authoritative Word of God. This blasphemous treatment of the Word of God does more harm than good. Just like people who go to churches with a very low view of scripture, students who take these courses end up not fearing the Lord and being inoculated against true Biblical Christianity.

The public schools claim that the content that they

teach is religiously neutral. Sadly, many Christian parents have fallen for that lie. The public school curriculum is designed to deliberately indoctrinate children into a morally relativistic, secular humanist worldview that is at war with Biblical Christianity.

Science classes replace God as Creator with a cosmic accident by teaching the Big Bang and Evolution as facts. Since they teach these unproven theories as facts, they also discredit the Bible's history regarding the creation of the universe and as a result, the reliability of the Bible as a whole. This is why many public school students believe evolution has disproven the Bible.

In addition, they replace the worship of the Creator with the worship of the creation by teaching extreme, leftwing, environmentalist propaganda, which culminates in the celebration of Earth Day. According to this view, human beings are not created in the image of God. Instead, they are the product of a freak accident in the primordial soup, the direct decedents of primates, without purpose in life except to live their lives for their own pleasure and self-fulfillment. As a result, human life and animal life are at best of equal value, and at worst humans are a cancer that must be removed from this world for the sake of the environment. "Save the whales!!! Kill the babies!!!" is their cry. In this view of the universe, at worst God doesn't exist or at best God set the universe in motion and left it to run by itself. Either way in this worldview, God is kicked off of His throne in place of man; and man becomes the supreme being of the universe with the "divine" right to determine what is true according to what seems right in his own eyes. In this worldview, man's word becomes supreme while God's Word is thrown in the garbage.

History classes follow this up by sanitizing the history books of Almighty God and any sign of Christianity's positive impact on modern civilization. Even though most of the primary documents from the founding fathers are full of references to God and direct quotes from the Bible demonstrating that our country was indeed founded upon Christian principles, the public school history curriculum pretends that these documents never existed. Liberal revisionist history for the purpose of political indoctrination is their goal. Instead of God being sovereign over history, they replace Him with the will of man. In addition, in these classes every religion is viewed as having equal value except "evil" Christianity; which happens to be the same position taken by the Roman Empire during the first 300 years of church history. The only time Christianity is mentioned is to highlight the arrogance and atrocities of the Crusades, the Inquisition, or the Salem Witch Trials, and to chastise Christians for trying to legislate morality while citing the ACLU's favorite myth of "the separation of church and state".

Many English classes continue the assault on Christianity by teaching students how to interpret literature from a deconstructionalist point of view. This process of interpretation typically involves demonstrating the multiple possible readings of a text and their resulting internal conflicts. With this view of textual interpretation, there is no objective way to interpret a text. This results in students who read asking themselves the question "What does the text mean to me?" instead of "What does the text actually mean?" As a result, when Christian public school students go to the Bible and approach its interpretation in the same way, they end up with the hermeneutical error of isogesis. This is when a reader's opinions are forced upon the scriptures resulting in the reader reading into the text whatever he wants the text to say, instead of using proper exegetical hermeneutics to find out what the text actually means. Isogesis not only results in an inaccurate interpretation of scripture, in addition, the reader also becomes guilty of placing his opinions in authority over God's Word, placing the opinions of a human being in authority over God Himself. This is a form of idolatry that has resulted and will continue to result in a plague of heresies within the church.

The illogical nature of deconstruction is simply an expression of the postmodern philosophy that dominates public education. This philosophy can be best described as a belief that there is no absolute truth, including no absolute moral truth. As a result, each individual person determines "truth" according to what seems right in his own eyes. Even though in itself the statement that absolute truth doesn't exist is self-contradictory and illogical because it is itself an absolute statement on the nature of truth, postmodernism is a logical result of the secular humanist worldview. By eliminating Almighty God from their worldview, they have eliminated the only possible source of absolute truth; and with no source for absolute truth, they conclude that absolute truth must not exist, and as a result, each individual person is left to determine truth for himself. The social repercussions of such a philosophy are either anarchy or totalitarianism, when for the sake of an orderly society the strong impose their "morality" and views of "truth" on the rest of the population. The moral repercussions are equally as horrible, moral relativism.

Moral relativism declares that good and evil don't exist, just different opinions that are equally true even if contradictory. In such a philosophy, the holocaust of the Jews and a person dying to save the lives of many are morally equal. No one could condemn the holocaust or praise self-sacrificing love because in postmodernism there is no absolute moral standard. There are only opinions coming from totally depraved human hearts that are in rebellion against Almighty God.

The fact that moral relativity has become the dominant ethical philosophy in the public schools is on full display in my classes during the bio-medical ethics seminar on embryonic stem cell research that I have my honor's biology students participate in each semester. Embryonic stem cell research consists of harvesting stem cells from human embryos that came from in-vitro fertilization clinics for the purpose of using these stem cells in an attempt to develop cures for a variety of human diseases. During the process, the human embryos are sacrificed for their stem cells. They are murdered in cold blood in the name of medical science. It would be like murdering a person on the street in order to harvest their organs for another person's organ transplant operation. Ultimately, this bio-medical ethics issue has the same ethical problem as abortion. Killing a human embryo is the murder of a genetically unique human being.

In my class, students spend several days doing research on both sides of the argument. They then write a 3 page research paper on the topic that includes why some people consider embryonic stem cell research to be ethical, why some people see it as the murder of human babies, and the position they have chosen including why they chose it. On the last day of the seminar, the students participate in an in-class debate involving the following 3 questions:

1. When do human beings receive their human right to life?
2. Do human beings come into existence with the inherent right to life or are human rights something that can be arbitrarily given or taken away by governments?
3. Is embryonic stem cell research ethical or unethical? Why?

During these debates the most disturbing ethical positions based on moral relativity have come to the surface. The following are several quotes from these debates:

"The medical experimentation that the Nazis conducted on the Jewish people during the holocaust would have to be considered ethical if it lead to cures for the German population."

"I would kill anyone in this room to harvest your organs if it meant I could save my dying mother!"

"If a person is not loved or wanted, we should be able to kill them for medical research."

During the debate, the ethical consistency of the student who was responsible for the last quote was challenged by the following question:

"If you were homeless (unloved and unwanted) and other people were in need of your organs, should they have the right to kill you and harvest your organs?"

The student responded with a bone chilling "Yes".

Throughout the years, comments such as these have become much more common. Moral relativity truly has become the norm in the public schools.

Besides teaching students to interpret literary works using deconstruction, English classes directly teach moral relativity through a 10th grade unit on cultural relativity. This is a unit where the morals and values of several distinct cultures are compared and contrasted for the purpose of proving that there is no such thing as an absolute moral standard. I recently overheard several English teachers talking about this unit during a staff development day. One of the teachers said the following:

"Some of my students walk into my class with definite ideas about what is right and wrong. But by the time they finish this unit they'll no longer be certain of anything."

Then another teacher chimed in, "They won't even be able to call what the Nazi's did during the holocaust evil."

In addition, many of the books that the students are assigned to read including many of the so called "classics" teach doctrines that are contrary to scripture or deliberately paint Biblical Christianity in a bad light. For example, Nathaniel Hawthorne's *The Scarlet Letter* raises the tolerance of sin to the level of a virtue and unjustly paints the Puritans, and in the mind of public schools students, all Christians as tyrannical, cruel, judgmental, and narrow-minded. In another example, they promote the works of Transcendentalists Thoreau and Emerson, and by doing so teach ideas that are similar to today's New Age spirituality. Ultimately, the themes that are presented in many of these books serve to lead students away from Biblical Christianity.

If this wasn't enough, secular psychology is at the core of every public school counseling department and school curriculum. This is one of the reasons that the public schools are not succeeding academically or socially. One of the biggest problems with secular psychology is that they start with a wrong view of human nature. They believe that human nature is inherently good and if you simply pump up their self-esteem and provide programs that spoon feed the students, they will succeed. In addition, if a student does not succeed, there is always an excuse. There is always a scapegoat. They blame the parents. They blame the teachers. But very rarely are the students truly held accountable. In the end, many students end up with an artificially inflated self-esteem, a sense of entitlement, and an aversion to taking responsibility for their actions. These are individuals who believe that they are good people that deserve to go to heaven regardless of the evidence to the contrary. This certainly increases the difficulty of witnessing to them with the gospel of Jesus Christ.

    In conclusion, after a close examination of the public school curriculum, it is obvious that the content that they teach is not religiously neutral. On the contrary, the public school curriculum tries to eliminate God, discredit the Bible, and deceive our children.

CHAPTER SIX:
The Public Schools and The Ten Commandments

The worldview that students end up with after being indoctrinated by the public school curriculum is of the devil. The rebellion and self-rule that is encouraged in this worldview results in students that delight in the breaking of the Ten Commandments that were given by God in Exodus 20: 1 - 17.

Commandment #1:
"You shall have no other gods before Me."

And

Commandment #2:
"You shall not make for yourself an idol."

The Big Bang Theory and Evolution are the public school's main weapons in their war against Almighty God. They use these unproven theories to try to eliminate God as their Creator. By providing a Godless alternative explanation to the origin of the universe, the origin of life, and the origin of humankind, they hope to prove to the world and ultimately to themselves that God is not necessary for their existence or sovereign over their lives. Ultimately, the purpose of these weapons are to eliminate God from the consciousness of man, so that man can feel free to sin to his heart's content without the fear of Divine judgment. As a result of buying into evolutionary theory, students end up breaking the first and second commandments by replacing God with themselves as they bow down to the idols of pleasure and self-fulfillment.

The following is a condensed version of the public school's Godless, secular humanist, creation story:

In the beginning there was nothing. Then out of nothing, a tiny dot came into existence. This dot was a singularity that contained all of the matter, space, time, and energy of the universe. Then suddenly, BANG!!! The dot rapidly expanded (the Big Bang). In the process, sub-atomic particles shooting out of the center of the singularity started to orbit each other forming the first hydrogen atoms. These hydrogen atoms collected in space forming giant gas clouds called nebula. The hydrogen atoms in these gas clouds squeezed together and became so dense that nuclear fusion was sparked, the birth of the first stars. Then through the process of nuclear fusion inside these stars, hydrogen atoms fused together to form helium atoms, and then the helium atoms fused together with other atoms to form heavier and heavier elements. And then bang!!! Some of these stars went super nova sending shockwaves and heavier elements to a neighboring gas cloud. As a result of the shockwaves, this gas cloud began to spin faster and faster and faster until the center became dense enough to spark nuclear fusion, the birth of our sun. The rest of the space debris then slammed together to become the planets, moons, asteroids, and comets of our solar system. (This is known as the nebular hypothesis that tries to explain the formation of our solar system.) Then a large sphere of molten rock orbiting the sun burped up water vapor. This water vapor then condensed into liquid water and rain came down on our planet for the first time. Time and time again the water kept evaporating, condensing, and precipitating until a thin, hard, rocky crust formed around our planet. As it kept raining, the water collected in the low areas that we now call the oceans. Then the residue of the rocks and the elements from the atmosphere collected in large quantities. Some think that this occurred on the surface of the ocean while others think that it happened at the bottom of the ocean. Either way, this soup of chemicals was given the name, the primordial soup. This soup is supposed to have contained proteins, carbohydrates, lipids, and nucleic acids, the compounds necessary for life. And then around 3.5 billion years ago, lightning struck and sparked the formation of the first life form. A living bag of goo emerged from the soup, the first living thing an anaerobic bacteria came into existence. The bacteria then decided to become more complex, gained brand new genetic information, and evolved into a protist. Then the protists evolved into invertebrates. Next, the invertebrates evolved into fish, and then fish into amphibians. Finally, amphibians evolved into reptiles, reptiles evolved into mammals, mammals evolved into primates, and primates evolved into you. That is cosmic and biological evolutionary theory in a nutshell; a sophisticated and elaborate fairytale for adults deliberately designed to free the human conscience from the sovereignty of God.

At this point in the discussion there is bound to be some readers who are under the false impression that evolution is a scientifically proven fact, and that God must have used the Big Bang and Evolution to create the universe and life as we know it. This false impression is understandable considering the fact that most Christians have gone through public school indoctrination and were raised in churches that trembled at the thought of challenging evolution. Thankfully, quite a few books have already been written that disprove evolution and illustrate how evolution is not compatible with a Biblical worldview. Nevertheless, I will attempt to summarize some of the main points.

Besides miracles, the origins issue is one of the only areas in which the Bible disagrees with modern science. But if you closely examine the claims of each and compare them to the <u>direct observation evidence</u>, the following three things become perfectly clear:

1. Evolutionists and Biblical creationists are both looking at the same exact physical evidence. They are looking at the same fossils, the same anatomical

structures, and the same DNA. The funny thing is that there is <u>zero</u> disagreement on what can be directly observed!!! Biblical creationists even believe that the directly observable process of natural selection was necessary to produce the many varieties of animal species within their kinds that exist today from the limited kinds of animals that were on Noah's ark.

2. The areas of disagreement are between the faith based philosophies that each use to interpret the physical evidence, not the evidence itself. Evolution interprets the evidence with a naturalistic (no God), uniformitarian, (the present is the key to the past) faith based philosophy. For example, evolutionary theory is based upon the faith based assumption that similar fossils, anatomy, and DNA prove that the animals and eventually people evolved from a common ancestor. The problem with the theory is that the only observable evidence is that living things are similar. Extrapolating that they evolved from a common ancestor is purely based on blind faith, not scientifically proven fact. Biological evolutionary theory has never been directly observed or verified by the scientific method.

On the other hand, Biblical creationists interpret the same evidence using the Bible as their ultimate authority. Biblical creationists look at the same exact evidence and declare that the similarities prove that they had a common Designer, Almighty

God. To be fair, this conclusion is also faith based. But having faith in what the Bible says is not blind faith at all, but faith in the all-knowing, all wise, and all powerful God who wrote it.

3. The Bible, being God's Word, is the standard of truth itself. As a result, it is not surprising that it has always been found to be consistent with what can be directly observed; while evolution contradicts direct observation evidence and violates several established scientific laws.

As the Word of God, the Bible in its original autographs is authoritative over all human knowledge. As a result, no apparent, perceived, or claimed evidence in any field of study, including science, history, and psychology, can be valid if it contradicts the Word of God. "For the wisdom of this world is foolishness with God."(1 Corinthians 3: 19a). God, knowing all things, can never be wrong; and since the Bible is the Word of God, the Bible can never be wrong. The Bible has demonstrated itself to be the Word of God by many infallible proofs such as 100% accuracy in the fulfillment of prophesies that were given hundreds of years before they were fulfilled, flawless historical and scientific accuracy, and the divine revelation of advanced, scientific knowledge thousands of years before being "discovered" by science.

In their attacks against the Bible in the area of science, skeptics have pointed out that the Bible is not a science book; and they are right. The Bible is not a science book.

However, everything that the Bible does say about scientific topics is 100% consistent with what can be directly observed and tested by the scientific method.

As stated earlier, the Bible contains many scientific facts that were undiscovered in the scientific community at the time that they were recorded in scripture. This documented phenomenon demonstrates the infallible, supernatural nature of the Bible. The following tables organized by scientific discipline illustrate this phenomenon:

BIOLOGY

The Bible says…	Direct Observation Evidence	Approximate Time it Took for Science to Catch up with the Bible
The blood clotting factor reaches its peak on Day #8 of life, perfect for circumcision. (Leviticus 12: 3)	The blood clotting factor reaches its peak on Day #8 of life, perfect for circumcision.	Over 3000 years
Blood is the source of life and health. (Leviticus 17:11)	Blood is the source of life and health by carrying oxygen and nutrients to your cells.	Over 3000 years

BIOLOGY continued...

The Bible says...	Direct Observation Evidence	Approximate Time it Took for Science to Catch up with the Bible
Blood from different races are compatible. (Acts 17: 26)	Blood from different races are compatible. (Common Blood Theory)	Almost 2000 years
Humans are all genetically related. (Genesis 3: 20)	Humans are all genetically related.	Almost 3500 years
Living things reproduce according to their kind. (Genesis 1: 21, 24 – 25)	Living things reproduce according to their kind.	Many Scientists still have not accepted the direct observation evidence. (3500 years and counting)

BIOLOGY continued...

The Bible says...	Direct Observation Evidence	Approximate Time it Took for Science to Catch up with the Bible
How to deal with Disease	All of these are based on Germ theory	
When dealing with disease, hands should be washed under running water. (Leviticus 15: 13)	When dealing with disease, hands should be washed under running water.	Over 3000 years
Isolate or even quarantine those who are sick. (Lev 13: 1 – 14: 57)	Isolate or even quarantine those who are sick.	Over 3000 years
Destroy contaminated objects and burn used dressings to prevent the spread of infection. (Leviticus 13: 1 – 14: 57; 11: 33, and 15: 12)	Destroy contaminated objects and burn used dressings to prevent the spread of infection.	Over 3000 years

ASTRONOMY

The Bible says...	Direct Observation Evidence	Approximate Time it Took for Science to Catch up with the Bible
The Earth is a Sphere. (Job 26: 10)	The Earth is a Sphere.	1500 years
The Earth Floats in Space. (Job 26: 7)	The Earth Floats in Space.	Almost 4000 years
The Universe is Expanding. (Isaiah 40: 22)	The Universe is Expanding.	Over 2500 years

CHEMISTRY AND PHYSICS

The Bible says…	Direct Observation Evidence	Approximate Time it Took for Science to Catch up with the Bible
No new matter can come into existence and no matter can be destroyed. (Genesis 2: 2, Hebrews 1: 3, Colossians 1: 17)	No new matter can come into existence and no matter can be destroyed (The First Law of Thermodynamics).	Over 1500 years
The entire universe is in a state of increasing decay or entropy. (Romans 8: 20 – 22)	The entire universe is in a state of increasing decay or entropy. (The Second Law of Thermodynamics)	Over 1500 years
Matter requires an invisible force to keep it together. (Col 1:17)	The nucleus of an atom requires an invisible nuclear force to hold it together.	Over 1500 years

EARTH SCIENCE

The Bible says...	Direct Observation Evidence	Approximate Time it Took for Science to Catch up with the Bible
"There are billions of dead things buried in rock layers that were laid down by water all over the Earth."[43] (Including on the Tops of Mountains) (Genesis 7: 19 – 22).	"There are billions of dead things buried in rock layers that were laid down by water all over the Earth." (Including on the Tops of Mountains) This is the fossil record.	1000 – 3000 years
The ocean floor contains deep valleys and mountains. (2 Samuel 22: 16)	The ocean floor contains deep valleys and mountains.	Almost 3000 years
The oceans contain springs. (Job 38: 16 and Genesis 7: 11)	The oceans contain springs (hydrothermal vents).	4000 years.

---

[43] Ken Ham, Founder and President of Answers in Genesis

These tables clearly demonstrate that in many cases, it has taken thousands of years for scientists to catch up with the advanced scientific concepts in the Bible. The truth is, scientists were wrong in their thinking for thousands of years and are wrong in their thinking in some areas to this very day. This is no insult to scientists, for they are only human. On the other hand, God, being omniscient, is never wrong. Each and every time the Word of God has been tested, it has demonstrated itself to be consistent with the direct observation evidence. This conclusion also holds true in the issue of origins.

When the Biblical account of creation and evolutionary theory (cosmic and biological) are compared to the direct observation evidence, an identical conclusion is inescapable. The Bible demonstrates itself to be consistent with what can be directly observed while evolution is left contradicting direct observation evidence and violating established scientific laws. The following table clearly demonstrates this conclusion:

THE ORIGINS ISSUE

The Direct Observation Evidence is ...	Is the Bible Consistent with the Direct Observation Evidence?	Is Cosmic and Biological Evolution Consistent with the Direct Observation Evidence?
The Universe is extremely complex.	Yes A brilliantly complex creation testifies to the existence of a brilliant Creator, just like a space shuttle testifies to the existence of aero-space engineers. (Romans 1: 20)	No Based on a naturalistic (no God) philosophy, Evolution looks at the obviously designed universe and blindly declares that it isn't really designed at all. Evolution declares that the universe's complexity is a result of random chance and time. This would be like believing that a tornado spinning through a junk yard could produce a space shuttle.

THE ORIGINS ISSUE continued...

The Direct Observation Evidence is ...	Is the Bible Consistent with the Direct Observation Evidence?	Is Cosmic and Biological Evolution Consistent with the Direct Observation Evidence?
The 1st Law of Thermodynamics states that matter cannot be created or destroyed.	Yes God being the Creator of matter. (Genesis1:1)	No The Big Bang Theory does not have an explanation for the origin of matter. They literally believe that matter came from nothing. This clearly goes against the 1st Law of Thermodynamics. You cannot get something from nothing!

THE ORIGINS ISSUE continued…

The Direct Observation Evidence is …	Is the Bible Consistent with the Direct Observation Evidence?	Is Cosmic and Biological Evolution Consistent with the Direct Observation Evidence?
The 2nd Law of Thermodynamics states that the universe is constantly increasing in Entropy/Disorder.	Yes. The universe is under the curse of the fall and is in a state of constant decay (Romans 8: 20 – 22)	No. Evolution requires the opposite. Evolution requires a consistent increase in the order and complexity of the universe. This requirement directly contradicts the 2nd Law of Thermodynamics. This required increase has never been directly observed.

THE ORIGINS ISSUE continued...

The Direct Observation Evidence is ...	Is the Bible Consistent with the Direct Observation Evidence?	Is Cosmic and Biological Evolution Consistent with the Direct Observation Evidence?
DNA is a language code that is more sophisticated than all of the computer programs that have ever been written put together. In addition, language codes and the information that they contain have only been observed to come from intelligent beings.	Yes God is the author of the DNA language code and the Origin of all information.	No Language codes and information have only been observed to come from intelligent beings, never from inanimate matter. Even though this is all that we have ever directly observed regarding information, evolution claims that the DNA language code and the information within originated from matter by random chance.

THE ORIGINS ISSUE continued...

The Direct Observation Evidence is ...	Is the Bible Consistent with the Direct Observation Evidence?	Is Cosmic and Biological Evolution Consistent with the Direct Observation Evidence?
Biogenesis: Life has only been observed to come from life.	Yes God is not only alive, but also the source of life. (Genesis 1)	No Even though spontaneous generation/life from non-life has never been observed in nature, has never been accomplished in the lab, and would never happen without the information in the DNA language code, evolution has blind faith that this has occurred.

THE ORIGINS ISSUE continued...

The Direct Observation Evidence is ...	Is the Bible Consistent with the Direct Observation Evidence?	Is Cosmic and Biological Evolution Consistent with the Direct Observation Evidence?
Living things consistently reproduce after their own kind. For example, bacteria have always been observed to produce bacteria, dogs always produce dogs, Humans always produce Humans etc...	Yes Living things reproduce according to their kind. (Genesis 1: 21, 24 – 25)	No Even though all that we have ever directly observed is living things reproducing after their own kinds, evolution claims that you evolved from bacteria. The evolution of one kind of organism from another has never been directly observed! In addition, this type of radical change would require the addition of massive amounts of new genetic information. This new genetic information would be needed as a biological blueprint for the brand new and much more complex biological engineering that evolution claims to produce. The problem for evolutionary theory is that genetic mutations have never been observed to add new genetic blueprint information for brand new, never seen before adaptations, only scramble or delete existing information.

Evolutionary theory is not consistent with the direct observation evidence when it comes to the existence of matter, entropy, genetic information, and the origin of life. In addition, evolutionary theory completely lacks any mechanism that could add the unimaginable amounts of new genetic information that would be needed to turn bacteria into you. Natural Selection shrinks gene pools by selecting genetic traits that already exist and genetic mutations have only been observed to scramble or loose genetic information resulting only in variations within a kind of organism. Given that evolutionary theory breaks several scientific laws and is not consistent with the direct observation evidence, why would so many scientists still hold onto this theory?

The following is what some high profile evolutionary scientists had to say:

"Everybody knows that organisms get better as they evolve. They get more advanced, more modern, and less primitive. And everybody knows that organisms get more complex as they evolve...

The only trouble with what everybody knows, says McShea, an evolutionary biologist at the University of Michigan, is that there is no evidence it's true."

(Dan McShae, "Onward and Upward?" by Lori Oliwenstein, Discover, June 1993, p. 22)

"I will not accept that [creation] philosophically, because I do not want to believe in God. Therefore, I choose to believe in

that which I know is scientifically impossible, spontaneous generation arising to evolution."

(George Wald [Nobel Prize winner], *"Biochemical Science: An Inquiry Into Life"*)

"Evolution is unproved and unprovable. We believe it only because the only alternative is special creation, and that is unthinkable."

(Sir Arthur Keith (he wrote the forward to the 100th anniversary edition of Darwin's book, Origin of Species in 1959)

When asked in a Television Interview "Why did the scientific community jump at Darwin's ideas?" Sir Julian Huxley – Head of UNESCO – one of the world's leading evolutionists said,

"I suppose the reason was why we leapt at the Origin of species was that the idea of God interfered with our sexual mores."

As you can see, high profile evolutionists don't believe in evolution because of their science. They believe in evolution because of their sin. They want to be the gods over their own lives so that they can sin to their hearts content. By believing in evolution, they break God's first and second commandments and open the door to the breaking of the rest. They practice this in their own lives and passionately indoctrinate students in the public schools to do the same.

For more information on the creation/evolution issue, please visit: http://www.answersingenesis.org/

Commandment #3: "You shall not take the name of the LORD your God in vain."

The public school curriculum eliminates God as Creator and Judge through the teaching of evolution and strips Him of His sovereignty over His creation through the teaching of liberal revisionist History. The result of this teaching is the complete absence of the fear of the LORD in the public schools. This is why public school students commonly use God's holy name as a filthy, four-letter word when they are angry, or use His name without the respect that it's due when they use it as a common expression to express surprise or wonderment. There is no fear of the LORD in their hearts even though God sees the taking of His name as filthy or common so seriously that King David said when singing to God in *Psalm 139: 20b: "your enemies take Your Name in vain!"* And God Himself declared in the Ten Commandments that on the Day of Judgment *"the LORD will not hold him guiltless who takes His Name in vain." (Exodus 20: 7b).* God sees a person who has taken His name in vain as a blasphemer and an enemy of God who will stand guilty on the Day of Judgment and yet, there is no fear of the LORD in the public schools.

Every time I witness to students outside of school, I begin with leading them through the Ten Commandments and teaching them about the Holiness and Justice of God in order to give them the fear of the LORD. This is a prerequisite for them so they will actually understand the good news of the gospel. Every time I do this, I find that my students have the greatest amount of apathy towards the 3rd commandment, and I am certain that along with the media, the public school curriculum plays a big role in encouraging this attitude.

Commandment#4: "Remember the Sabbath day, to keep it holy."

God instituted The Sabbath long before the Mosaic Law was given. After He created the universe in six 24 hour days, God blessed the seventh day and made it holy (Genesis 2: 3). The 4th Commandment instructs us to set aside one day in seven as a day of rest from our worldly employment. On that one day out of seven, we are called to focus all of our energies on the public and private worship of God (Exodus 20:8-11; Nehemiah 13:15-22; Isaiah 58:13-14; Revelation 1:10), and on duties of necessity and mercy (Matthew 12:1-13 and Mark 2:27-28).

When it comes to keeping the Christian Sabbath holy, the American culture has strayed a long way from the days of the blue laws. I believe that this is also a direct result of a lack of the fear of the LORD which is encouraged by the public school curriculum.

People need to remember that in the Old Testament, God judged the breaking of the Sabbath just as severely as He judged idolatry and other heinous transgressions of the moral law (Ezekiel 20:13, Ezekiel 20: 16 – 21,

Nehemiah 13:18, and Jeremiah 17:19-27). God took the breaking of this commandment very seriously, and at first, so did the Israelites. But as time went by, Jewish religious leaders corrupted the Sabbath by adding many man-made rules.

In the New Testament, Jesus did not come to do away with the moral law; He came to fulfill it (Matthew 5; 17 – 19). Since keeping the Sabbath day holy is part of the moral law, Jesus didn't come to do away with the Sabbath as some claim, but instead to reform the Sabbath as the LORD of the Sabbath (Matthew 12: 1 – 14, Mark 2:27). Jesus even took for granted that the Sabbath would still be kept after His death and resurrection when He prophesized about the abomination of desolation (Matthew 24: 15 – 22). In addition, Isaiah 66: 22 – 23 contains a prophesy about eternity future that has God using Sabbaths to mark time. A strong case can be made from these scriptures that Jesus wanted the apostles to keep the Sabbath day holy even after He ascended to heaven. And this is exactly what the apostles did, with the exception of changing the day. Under the guidance of the Holy Spirit, the apostles changed the Sabbath to the first day of the week (Sunday); and called it the Lord's Day in commemoration of Jesus' Resurrection (John 20:1, Acts 20:7, 1 Corinthians 16:2, Revelation 1:10). Afterward, the apostle Paul made it clear that we should not judge each other over what day we choose to celebrate the Sabbath (Romans 14:5-6, Colossians 2:16-17). But the majority of the early Christian church chose to celebrate the Sabbath on the Lord's Day, as have many churches since.

Since this is the Biblical history of the 4th Commandment, the celebration of the Lord's Day as the Christian Sabbath should be taken seriously. But the public schools are so far removed from fearing the LORD, that they could care less about keeping the Christian Sabbath holy. They have such disregard for the 4th Commandment that my school even had their high school graduation on a Sunday morning.

In general, people with a God hating, morally relativistic, secular humanist worldview look at the Christian Sabbath, in the same way as Bill Gates:

"Just in terms of allocation of time resources, religion is not very efficient. There's a lot more I could be doing on a Sunday morning."

Do your children have this attitude toward the preaching of God's Word on Sunday morning? If they do, thank the public schools.

Commandment#5: "Honor your father and your mother."

There are three reasons for why this commandment seems like a joke to the average public high school student. First, most public school raised children don't have strong personal relationships with their parents. We are in a culture that has mastered the art of dividing the family. During the week they are divided by work, school, and extra-curricular activities. On Sundays they are divided by age-segregated programs at church. Even at home they are divided by the many individualized entertainment choices that are available (TV, internet, video games, phone calls, texting etc...). In the end, generally speaking, children raised in our society don't know their parents and their parents don't know them. They are like roommates who share living arrangements in the same house, but live completely different individualized lives. As a result, the idea of honoring their parents normally doesn't cross the mind of the average public school student.

Second, they spend the majority of their childhood not receiving Biblical discipline from their parents. Even if parents believe in using Biblical discipline and occasionally train their children, because their children are away from them in the public schools for most of the day, proper Biblical character development is stunted. And most of the time, the result is exactly what the book of Proverbs says:

> *"The rod and rebuke give wisdom,*
> *But a child left to himself brings shame to his mother." (Proverbs 29: 15) (NKJV)*

The last reason that most public school students don't take this commandment seriously is because of the media they consume and the student culture that they are immersed in for at least 7 hours a day, 5 days a week, 180 days a year! The media that most children in America consume strongly encourages rebellion against authority, especially the authority of parents. From a very young age, starting with something as seemingly innocent as cartoons, children are being brainwashed with the attitude that it is ok to break the 5th Commandment. This attitude is further reinforced when the children are sent to the public schools and are surrounded by peers who glory in rebellion. The longer the children remain in the public schools, the more convinced they become that dishonoring their parents with a rebellious, sassy attitude is no big deal. It is just being a normal kid. Sadly, even most church going adults don't see the breaking of this commandment as a big deal, but God does.

According to God, children are supposed to honor their parents by obeying them in everything as onto the LORD (Ephesians 6: 1), right away, and with a good attitude. If you do not think that God is serious about this commandment, read the following list that describes people who deserve God's Wrath:

> *"They are full of envy, <u>murder</u>, strife, deceit, maliciousness. They are gossips, slanderers, <u>haters of God</u>, insolent, haughty, boastful, inventors of evil, <u>disobedient to parents</u>, foolish, faithless, heartless, ruthless." (Romans 1: 29b – 31)(Emphasis added)*

"Disobedient to parents" is on the same list, side by side with "murder" and "haters of God".

The reason for God taking the 5th Commandment this seriously is because God has determined that the family, especially the husband and wife relationship, is a visible picture to the world of the relationship between Christ and His church, with Christ being represented by the husband and the church being represented by the wife.

> *"Husbands, love your wives, as Christ loved the church and gave Himself up for her, that He might sanctify her, having cleansed her by the washing of water with the word, so that He might present the church to Himself in splendor, without spot or wrinkle or any such thing, that she might be holy and without blemish. In the same way husbands should love their wives as their own bodies. He who loves his wife loves himself. For no one ever hated his own flesh, but nourishes and cherishes it, just as Christ does the church, because we are members of His body. "Therefore a man shall leave his father and mother and hold fast to his wife, and the two shall become one flesh." This mystery is profound, and I am saying that it refers to Christ and the church. However, let each one of you love his wife as himself, and let the wife see that she respects her husband." (Ephesians 5: 25 – 33)*

With the following being the role of the children:

> *"Children, obey your parents in the Lord, for this is right. 'Honor your father and mother' (this is the first commandment with a promise), 'that it may go well with you and that you may live long in the land.'" (Ephesians 6: 1 – 3)*

As a result, when a child dishonors his parents, he is dishonoring the representation of Christ to the world, rebelling against the authority of God Himself.

In the end, it is obvious that God cares about children honoring their parents as onto the Lord, and that the practice of sending children to the public schools encourages the breaking of the 5th Commandment.

Commandment #6: "You shall not murder."

What is more like God: An angel, you, or a worm? The answer is; none of them. God is holy. He is completely unique, distinct, and separate from His creation. The difference between you and God is not just quantitative, it is qualitative. God isn't just infinitely bigger and more powerful than you are, God isn't just infinitely smarter, more knowledgeable, and wiser than you are; God is in a completely different qualitative category than you. He is the Creator; you are just a tiny part of His creation. God is Eternal, Self-Existing, and Unchanging. God is the Alpha and the Omega (Revelation 1: 8)!!!

While God is infinite and eternal, you are finite; and your life is like a vapor, here today and gone tomorrow (James 4: 14). God has no beginning and no end. God Himself is the beginning of all things (Revelation 21: 6, 22: 13). He created the universe out of nothing and sustains it with His Almighty power (Genesis 1: 1, Hebrews 1: 3), while you cannot add a single hour to your life or even make one of your hairs white or black (Matthew 5: 36). Even a majestic Angel of God who has the power to slay an army of human soldiers in one night, as a part of God's creation is as much like God as a worm. Since this is the case, what does that make you compared to God?

The answer to this question is obvious and the ramifications are startling. We have no value, no worth, and no rights unless God Himself gives them to us; but thankfully He has. Almighty God has given human beings immeasurable value by creating us in His image on the sixth day of creation.

"Then God said, "Let Us make man in Our image, after Our likeness. And let them have dominion over the fish of the sea and over the birds of the heavens and over the livestock and over all the earth and over every creeping thing that creeps on the earth."
So God created man in His own image,
in the image of God He created him;
male and female He created them." (Genesis 1: 26 – 27)

What this means is that God (Father, Son, and Holy Spirit), in His Sovereign will, decided to make us His image bearers. It is this fact that makes murder such a diabolically evil act. When talking to Noah after God's judgment of the global flood, God said:

> *"And for your lifeblood I will require a reckoning: from every beast I will require it and from man. From his fellow man I will require a reckoning for the life of man. "Whoever sheds the blood of man, by man shall his blood be shed, <u>for God made man in His own image</u>." (Genesis 9: 5 – 6)(Emphasis added)*

    It is the image of God that gives us immeasurable value. It is the image of God that makes every single human life, from the moment of conception to the moment of their God determined death, sacred.

    But according to the public schools' evolutionary, secular humanist worldview, human beings were not created in the image of God. Instead, they are the product of a freak accident in the primordial soup, the direct decedents of primates, without any inherent special value, worth, or rights. This is why secular humanists believe that an animal's life is of equal of greater value than a human's life. Many humanists will go as far as saying that humans are a cancer that must be removed from this world for the sake of the environment. This is the message that our children are being indoctrinated with by both the media and the public schools. This is why human life is no longer sacred in our society.

    Murder is glorified in movies, TV, music, and especially in first-person shooter video games where children act out the murder of human beings countless times from a first person perspective. This has bred a hatred for fellow human beings in our children and has encouraged children to break the 6th Commandment countless times by murdering in their hearts without any remorse. The Bible clearly states:

> "**Everyone who hates his brother is a murderer**, and you know that no murderer has eternal life abiding in him."
> *(1 John 3: 15)(Emphasis added)*

This is a serious crime against God because since we were created in His image, hatred towards our fellow human beings is hatred towards God Himself.

Sadly, one way or another, the fruits of this hatred have a tendency to come out of the heart. This is exactly what happened at the Columbine high school massacre and in the millions of incidences of school violence that have occurred in the past decade. As Jesus said:

> "**For out of the heart come** evil thoughts, **murder**, adultery, sexual immorality, theft, false witness, slander." *(Matthew 15: 18 – 20)*

Our culture is the epitome of hypocrisy. We rightly view Hitler as a monster because he ordered the murder of 6 million Jews during the holocaust, yet we think we are a morally "good" even though according to the Guttmacher Institute, from 1973 through the present, the American culture has been in the midst of a massive holocaust of its own.

God declares that human life begins at conception (Jeremiah 1:4-5, Psalm 139:13-16). Modern Science agrees and states that a human life that is genetically distinct from his parents begins when a sperm fertilizes the egg. In spite of this, the worldview of the American media and the public schools has indoctrinated students with a culture that minimizes the miracle of life and champions the right of mothers to choose death for their unborn babies.

From 1973 to 2008 our culture legally murdered nearly 50 million unborn babies in cold blood, and millions have been murdered since. It has gotten so bad that abortion is now the leading cause of death in America:

33% abortion
16% heart disease
15% cancer
36% all other causes
(based on 2011 statistics from Guttmacher Institute and Centers for Disease Control)[44]

In addition, twenty-two percent of all pregnancies (excluding miscarriages) end in abortion, and at current rates, 1 in 10 women will have an abortion by age 20, 1 in 4 by age 30, and 3 in 10 by age 45.[45]

These statistics reflect the general attitude that exists within the public school student culture. The idea of

---

[44] Answers Magazine, Vol. 8 No. 2, April – June 2013, p. 13.
[45] Guttmacher Institute

abortion as just another birth control option as they live their lives of fornication is common among my students. To many of them, murdering their unborn babies is preferable to taking responsibility for their actions. Many teenage boys see abortion as their "get out of jail free card" from the responsibility of fatherhood and as a license to pursue a promiscuous lifestyle; while many of the teenage girls see abortion as a feminist right and the key to liberate themselves from the "shackles" of motherhood. Their contempt for life and their commitment to fornication is almost palpable.

A couple of times during my career, my wife and I begged teenage mothers to let us adopt their babies instead of killing them by having an abortion. As God willed, each time we made our plea caused the mothers to reconsider motherhood. I suppose that seeing someone else sincerely want their babies made them realize just how precious their babies really were. We are thankful to God that He placed us at the right place and time to stop those abortions; but our hearts are broken over the fact that there are countless abortions happening all around us that we are unable to prevent. The American holocaust continues.

The United States of America has truly become a culture of death, and this is only the beginning. With the financial "burden" of a larger percentage of the population entering retirement within the next couple of decades coupled with the reduction of the number of people entering the workforce to finance their social security retirement, the euthanizing of the elderly will become our next holocaust. This is the logical fruit of the God hating worldview that our children are being indoctrinated with as they partake of the poison that is public education. As God said, *"all who hate Me love death." (Proverbs 8: 36b)* And if you understand the 6th Commandment the reverse is also true, all who love death hate God.

Commandment#7: "You shall not commit adultery."

Many of my students try to escape the guilt of breaking this commandment by claiming that since they are not married, this commandment doesn't apply to them. They couldn't be more wrong. God sees all sexual activity outside of marriage as sexual immorality. Jesus even said that if you look upon a person to lust after them, you have already committed adultery with them in your heart (Matt. 5: 27 – 28). This means that the breaking of this commandment would include adultery, pre-marital sex, homosexual sex, or having sexual thoughts about someone who is not your spouse, including viewing pornography. A person's marital status is irrelevant.

God sees these infractions of His law as serious crimes because they violate the doctrine of marriage. God established the sacrament of marriage in the Garden of Eden as a covenant between one man and one woman where by entering into this covenant, they would become one flesh.

> *"So the Lord God caused a deep sleep to fall upon the man, and while he slept took one of his ribs and closed up its place with flesh. And the rib that the Lord God had taken from the man He made into a woman and brought her to the man. Then the man said, "This at last is bone of my bones and flesh of my flesh; she shall be called Woman, because she was taken out of Man." Therefore a man shall leave his father and his mother and hold fast to his wife, and they shall become one flesh."* (Genesis 2: 21 – 24)

In addition, God established marriage as a representation of Christ's relationship with the church, with Christ being represented by the husband and the church being represented by the wife. As a result, every kind of sexual immorality (adultery, pre-marital sex, homosexual sex, having sexual thoughts about someone who is not your spouse, viewing pornography etc...) is not just a sin against your spouse or your future spouse it is also a direct assault on the image of Christ's relationship with the church. Unfortunately, these things are of no concern to those who have been indoctrinated into the culture of sexual debauchery that is acted out daily in the public schools.

As was discussed earlier, public school students have made the breaking of this commandment their most glorified extracurricular activity. They glory in the marring of the image of Christ's relationship with the church without even knowing it. This is to be expected when God is taken out of the picture and the purpose of life is presented as self-fulfillment and the unquenchable pursuit of pleasure instead of the glory of God. As a result, fornication of all kinds has risen almost to the level of a "God given" right in the minds of public school students.

Due to decades of secular humanist indoctrination, the public schools have been churning out generations of people who are more and more accepting of what the Bible calls an abomination, the homosexual lifestyle. Based on their worldview, homosexuals should have the same right to pursue pleasure and self-fulfillment as heterosexual fornicators.

On the other hand, contrary to the secular humanist worldview, God clearly states that homosexuality is an abomination.

"You shall not lie with a male as with a woman; it is an abomination." (Leviticus 18: 22)

"Therefore God gave them up in the lusts of their hearts to impurity, to the dishonoring of their bodies among themselves, because they exchanged the truth about God for a lie and worshiped and served the creature rather than the Creator, who is blessed forever! Amen. For this reason God gave them up to <u>dishonorable passions. For their women exchanged natural relations for those that are contrary to nature; and the men likewise gave up natural relations with women and were</u>

> *consumed with passion for one another, men committing shameless acts with men and receiving in themselves the due penalty for their error. And since they did not see fit to acknowledge God, God gave them up to a debased mind to do what ought not to be done." (Romans 1: 24 – 28)(Emphasis added)*
>
> *"Or do you not know that the unrighteous will not inherit the kingdom of God? Do not be deceived: neither the sexually immoral, nor idolaters, nor adulterers, nor men who practice homosexuality, nor thieves, nor the greedy, nor drunkards, nor revilers, nor swindlers will inherit the kingdom of God."*
> *(1 Corinthians 6: 9 – 10)(Emphasis added)*

Considering what God says in His Word makes the national trend towards accepting homosexuality as a morally acceptable alternative lifestyle all the more disturbing. According to Gallup's national Values and Beliefs survey of 2007, 57% of Americans believed that homosexuality was an acceptable alternative lifestyle up from 38% in 1992.

Year	% of Americans That See Homosexuality as an Acceptable Alternative Lifestyle
1992	38%
1996	44%
1997	42%
1999	50%
2001	52%
2002	51%
2003	54%
2004	54%
2005	51%
2006	54%
2007	57%

[46]

The percentage of Americans that see homosexuality as an acceptable alternative lifestyle has consistently and dramatically increased from one generation to the next

The 2007 data also resulted in the following generational breakdown that predicted that this percentage would continue to increase in the future.

The Percentage of Americans That See Homosexuality as an Acceptable Alternative Lifestyle in 2007 Broken Down by Age Group

---

[46] Gallup's National Values and Beliefs Survey of 2007

Age Groups	% of Americans That See Homosexuality As Acceptable
18-34 years	75%
35- 54 years	58%
55+ years	45%

With 75% of 18-34 year-olds seeing the homosexual lifestyle as an acceptable alternative compared to just 45% of people of 55+ years of age, it is obvious that the secular humanist indoctrination in the public schools has been working. And with the majority of children being indoctrinated into this liberal worldview by the public schools with the help of the media and the reinforcement of their peer group, it is not hard to imagine a future where the United States of America becomes a modern day Sodom and Gomorrah, if it isn't already.

Gallup stopped asking this exact question in 2008, but the results of another question makes it clear that since the 2007 study the situation has gotten much worse. When asked the question, "Do you personally believe gay or lesbian relations are morally acceptable or morally wrong?" the percentage of people that believe that homosexuality is morally acceptable went up from 47% in 2007 to 56% in 2011, with the 56% being an all-time high. At the same time, the percentage of people that believe homosexuality is morally wrong went from 49% in 2007 to only 39% in 2011, with the 39% being a new all-time low.

Do You Personally Believe Gay or Lesbian Relations Are Morally Acceptable or Morally Wrong?

Year	Morally Acceptable	Morally Wrong
2007	47%	49%
2011	56%	39%

This is almost a 20% shift in the national attitude in favor of homosexuality in only 4 years. In 2007, people who believed that homosexuality was morally wrong were still in the majority by 2%. But in 2011, people who believe that homosexuality is morally acceptable now hold a commanding majority by 17%. Welcome to Sodom and Gomorrah!

I would like to take a moment to consider what homosexuality represents and what our response to homosexuality should be. We know that homosexuality is seen by God as an abomination (Leviticus 18: 22). As described in Romans 1: 24 – 28, homosexuality is the most extreme form of sexual immorality. It is when God stops restraining sexual sin as a result of idolatry. It is when God allows a person's totally depraved nature take over in the area of sexual sin. Even though this is the case, as ambassadors of God charged to deliver His message of reconciliation (2 Corinthians 5: 17 – 20), we must resist the self-righteous urge to demonize homosexuals above other sinners. Instead, as God's ambassadors, we need to approach homosexuals with the gospel centered, humble spirit, of compassion and love. Our chief motivation in our God given ministry of reconciliation is our love for God and our love for our fellow man as stated in the greatest commandment:

> *"And you shall love the Lord your God with all your heart and with all your soul and with all your mind and with all your strength. 'The second is this: 'You shall love your neighbor as yourself.' There is no other commandment greater than these." (Mark 12: 30 –31)*

The glory of God is our primary aim for evangelism. The reason for this is because of the love of God that He expressed for us on the cross. As a result of His love, we now love God more than anything in the universe including our own lives. As a result, we want nothing more than to see Him worshiped, that our loving Savior may receive the reward of His suffering. This is followed by the ultimate expression of our love for our neighbors as we seek to save them from the same eternity in hell that we deserved because of our sins before Jesus saved us.

> *"Or do you not know that the unrighteous will not inherit the kingdom of God? Do not be deceived: <u>neither the sexually immoral, nor idolaters, nor adulterers, nor men who practice homosexuality</u>, nor thieves, nor the greedy, nor drunkards, nor revilers, nor swindlers will inherit the kingdom of God. <u>And such were some of you. But you were washed, you were sanctified, you were</u>*

> ***justified in the name of the Lord Jesus Christ and by the Spirit of our God."*** *(1 Corinthians 6: 9 – 11)*
> *(Emphasis added)*

This passage makes it very clear that Jesus died for the sexual immorality of both heterosexuals and homosexuals alike. Just like Jesus loved us while we were still His enemies (Romans 5: 8 – 11) Jesus loves the elect among the homosexual community. In addition, just as Jesus is more than capable of cleansing us from all sin and empowering us to repent of any sin, Jesus is more than capable of regenerating the hearts of homosexuals, causing them to hate the homosexuality they once loved, and repent of the homosexual lifestyle. As a result, as Jesus' ambassadors, we are called to love homosexuals just as Jesus loved us by delivering the message of reconciliation, the gospel of Jesus Christ, and teaching them everything that He has commanded (Matthew 28: 18 – 20).

Ultimately, the rise in the acceptance of homosexually in our culture should drive us to preach the gospel to the homosexual community and protect our children from public school indoctrination. Since we know that the public schools indoctrinate students into a worldview that believes that the homosexual lifestyle is morally acceptable, we should remove our children from the public schools and encourage others to do likewise.

Commandment#8: **"You shall not steal."**

And

Commandment#9: "You shall not lie."

The 2010 Josephson Institute of Ethics' surveyed the values and ethical actions of more than 40,000 public and private high school students, with a specific focus on stealing, lying, and cheating. Almost one in three boys (33%) and one in four girls (25%) admitted stealing from a store within the past year. More than eight in ten (80%) confessed that they have lied to a parent about something significant. A majority of students (59 %) admitted cheating on a test during the last year, with 34 percent doing it more than two times, and one in three (33%) admitted they used the internet to plagiarize an assignment.

The blatant lack of integrity of this generation is the logical outcome of the moral relativism that is preached by the media and taught in the public schools. This postmodern approach to ethics always results in a moral code where the ends justify the means. And if the ultimate end for most people with this worldview is their own self-fulfillment and pleasure, from their point of view, it would be moral to use any means necessary to accomplish their ends. Related to this, moral relativism also results in a situational ethics view of good and evil. In this view, the situation a person is in would determine whether what a person does is good or evil. With this view, it is possible for obvious evils like cold blooded murder, adultery, theft, lying, and cheating to be viewed as morally good if it accomplishes what they would consider to be a "good" end. This is how these students justify using evil means in the name of self-fulfillment, or even justify calling what is obviously evil good.

> *"Though they know God's righteous decree that those who practice such things deserve to die, they not only do them but give approval to those who practice them."*
> *(Romans 1: 32)*

In their worldview there is no absolute standard of good and evil, no absolute moral law to judge their thoughts, words, and actions. Their state of mind is the epitome of moral and ethical chaos; everyone feeling justified in doing what is right in their own eyes, while firmly believing they are "good" people regardless of what they have done.

Even though the majority of these students demonstrated an undeniable lack of integrity, 92 % were completely satisfied with their personal ethics and character, which is exactly what the Word of God would predict.

> *"Most men will proclaim each his own goodness,"*
> *(Proverbs 20: 6b)*

The combination of moral relativity and self-righteousness has resulted in my students feeling no shame when they have been caught cheating. Stealing a good grade and lying to everyone about it doesn't seem like a big deal to them; but it is a big deal to God. God declares that no thief will have their part in the kingdom of God (1 Corinthians 6: 9 – 10), and that all liars will have their part in the lake of fire (Revelation 21: 8).

When hearing this during a witnessing encounter outside of school, my students quickly proclaim that "everybody lies". They don't seem to understand why lying would be such a serious crime to God. Well, let's take a closer look to find out.

Jesus called Himself the Truth. Jesus said, *"I am the way, and <u>the truth</u>, and the life. No one comes to the Father except through me."* *(John 14: 6b)(Emphasis added)* Truth is in the very Character of God, while lying is in the very character of Satan.

> *"He (Satan) was a murderer from the beginning, and has nothing to do with the truth, because there is no truth in him. <u>When he lies, he speaks out of his own character, for he is a liar and the father of lies.</u>" (John 8: 44b) (Emphasis and Explanation added)*

Since this is the case, it is easy to see why God hates lying and declares in His Word that *"Lying lips are an abomination to the LORD," (Proverbs 12:22)* and that all liars will have their part in the lake of fire (Revelation 21: 8).

When people lie, they violate the very Character of God and behave like a child of the devil (John 8: 43 – 45).

I pray that God uses explanations like these to

convict my students' hearts so that when they hear the gospel, they will repent of their sins and trust Jesus as their Lord and Savior.

Commandment #10: "You shall not covet."

The tenth commandment declares that we should never desire something that belongs to someone else. The reason for this is that when we covet something that does not belong to us, we are declaring that God Himself is unfair in not giving us what we want. When we do this, we are throwing a fit like spoiled children who are not thankful for what God as already provided. A covetous heart, if left unchecked, becomes a heart that is consumed with envy and greed. In the end, a covetous heart becomes a heart that casts God out and seeks after idols.

> *"Put to death therefore what is earthly in you: sexual immorality, impurity, passion, evil desire, <u>and covetousness, which is idolatry</u>.*
> *(Colossians 3: 5)(Emphasis added)*

Covetousness is idolatry! Covetousness also happens to be one of the main character traits of children raised in the public schools.

Since the public school curriculum removes God as the Creator and Judge, and encourages students to be the gods over their own lives, the public school curriculum opens the door wide for the practice of idolatry. This is manifested in a covetousness that almost rises to the level of insanity. They have a maniacal obsession with self-fulfillment and an unquenchable thirst for pleasure.

Whatever a person lives for is their idol and their god. If a person lives for their own pleasure (sex, drugs, pornography, drunkenness, entertainment etc…), then pleasure is their idol. If a person lives for money, then money is their idol. If a person lives for their own self-fulfillment and happiness, then self-fulfillment and happiness is their idol. Even if a person lives for their own children, then their children have become their idol. That is why God tested Abraham's faithfulness in the way that He did in Genesis 22: 1 - 19. God does not allow the worship of anything but HIMSELF. But sadly, the public schools encourage the worship of anything but HIM.

Ultimately, by encouraging the breaking of the Ten Commandments, the public schools will be judged by God as those who deserve worse than having a millstone hung around their necks and tossed into the sea.

> As Jesus said, *"but whoever causes one of these little ones who believe in me to sin, it would be better for him to have a great millstone fastened around his neck and to be drowned in the depth of the sea.*
> *"Woe to the world for temptations to sin! For it is necessary that temptations come, but woe to the one by whom the temptation comes!"* (Matthew 18: 6 – 7)

CHAPTER SEVEN:
The Public Schools and the Gospel

The public schools not only encourage the breaking of every single one of the Ten Commandments, they also keep out and systematically sabotage the only information that can save these students from an eternity in hell, the gospel of Jesus Christ. The following table summarizes how the public school curriculum accomplishes this demonic act.

NECESSARY ELEMENTS OF THE GOSPEL	HOW PUBLIC SCHOOL INDOCTRINATION SABOTAGES THE GOSPEL
God is the Creator and Sovereign Judge of the universe.	Public school science classes teach The Big Bang Theory and Evolution. In addition, history classes remove God as being sovereign over the events of history. God has no place in their history except to be scorned and mocked. This means that no God is needed as Creator and Sovereign Judge.

NECESSARY ELEMENTS OF THE GOSPEL	HOW PUBLIC SCHOOL INDOCTRINATION SABOTAGES THE GOSPEL
The Bible is God's Word: God determines absolute truth.	Since God doesn't exist, there is no absolute truth as taught by post modernism. As a result, man determines truth for himself. Since there is no God according to evolution, the Bible must have been written by flawed power hungry men. Either way, evolution proves the creation account in Genesis wrong. Since the Bible is wrong in Genesis, you can't trust any of it. In addition, English and history classes teach how Christianity is a manmade religion that can't be trusted because it has been used to oppress people throughout history. In the end, the Bible is a flawed book written by men to oppress people. As a result, I am the one who determines truth for myself.
The Fall: Adam and Eve's rebellion resulted in original sin and the total depravity of the human race.	Since evolution is true, Adam and Eve never existed and as a result, original sin does not exist. In addition, since psychology is true, I am a good person who deserves to have a good self-esteem.

NECESSARY ELEMENTS OF THE GOSPEL	HOW PUBLIC SCHOOL INDOCTRINATION SABOTAGES THE GOSPEL
God's Law: By breaking God's Law we are guilty of sin and deserve an eternity in hell.	Since God doesn't exist, there is no such thing as an absolute moral law. The philosophy of moral relativism is true. As a result, sin is a figment of people's overactive imaginations and there is no such thing as divine judgment.
Substitutionary Atonement and the Resurrection: Jesus Christ, the Creator of the universe showed His infinite love for us by dying on the cross to save us from the penalty of our sins and on the third day, He rose from the dead.	Since God doesn't exist, we are inherently good, and the Bible is hopelessly flawed, we don't have to fear judgment, we can sin to our hearts content, and we are in no need of a Savior. The End result: Jesus Christ as presented in the Bible is an unnecessary myth.
Gospel Call: In response to His incredible kindness, repent of your sins and trust in Jesus Christ as your Lord and Savior.	Foolishness!!!

CHAPTER EIGHT:
It is Time for Christian Parents to Abandon the Public Schools

It is time to come to terms with the stark contrast between a Biblical education and a public education. The public schools violate all 6 commands and principles that make up a Biblical education. The public schools encourage the breaking of the Ten Commandments, and systematically sabotage the message of the gospel. The following is a brief recap of the 6 commands and principles which God has laid out for us regarding how we should educate our children, along with a brief commentary which summarizes why Christian parents cannot fulfill these Biblical principles when they send their children to the public schools.

As you read this, please pray to God for the wisdom to be able to see public education for what it really is and for the conviction to do whatever it takes to remove your children from the public schools.

Principle#1: Education belongs to the family supported by the church, not to the state. [47]

Fathers are commanded to bring their children up in the discipline and instruction of the LORD with mothers as their primary helpers and with the support of the church. (Ephesians 6: 4, Psalm 78:5-8, and Deuteronomy 6: 1 - 7) (Genesis 2: 18 – 24, Proverbs 1:8, Proverbs 6:20, Song of Solomon 8:2, Acts 16: 1, and 2 Timothy 1: 5) (Ephesians 4: 11 – 16).

According to the U.S. First and Ninth Circuit Courts of Appeals, in the public schools the state determines what the children will be taught, not the father. In addition, the father doesn't even have the legal right to have his children opted out of subject matter that he finds objectionable. His parental rights stop at the schoolhouse door.[48] This fact makes it impossible for parents to fulfill this Biblical principle when they send their children to the public schools.

Principle#2: Do not be unequally yoked with unbelievers. (2 Corinthians 6: 14 – 18)

The public schools are temples of secular humanism that specialize in indoctrinating our children into a God

---

[47] Exodus Mandate, "Education belongs to the family, supported by the church, and not to the state",
July 17, 2012
[48] Michael P. Farris, J.D., A Dangerous Path, Has America Abandoned Parental Rights?, *reprinted from* The Home School Court Report *(vol. XXII, no. 4))*

hating secular humanist worldview. Sending our children to the public schools would be the same as first century Christians sending their children to Roman schools where they would learn to worship Caesar, sacrifice to a pantheon of pagan gods, and ultimately hate the Christian church. The practice of sending our children to the public schools is a clear violation of this Biblical principle.

Principle#3: Teachers must have a godly character because a student will become like his teacher. (Luke 6: 39 – 40, and Psalm 1)

Most public school teachers are not born again Christians with a commitment to teaching a Biblical worldview. Even most teachers who are Christians choose to participate in the secular humanist indoctrination of their students. Placing our children at the feet of the wicked, the sinners, and the scoffers will be and has been a curse to our children (Psalm 1). As Jesus said, *"everyone when he is fully trained will be like his teacher." (Luke 6: 40b)*

Principle#4: Bad company really does corrupt good character. (Proverbs 13: 20) (1 Corinthians 15: 33)

The Word of God and the testimony of experience verify that bad company really does corrupt good character and that children are truly more vulnerable to than mature adults. If you add these truths to hat the public school student culture is toxic, you end up with a recipe for disaster. The following is a summary of all of the studies concerning the public school student culture that have been quoted in this book for the purpose of reminding us of just how toxic this student culture really is:

Out of an average 30 student high school class, 15 would be sexually active[49], 23 would believe that homosexuality is an acceptable alternative lifestyle[50], 14 don't see a great risk in heavy daily drinking, 12 of them have used marijuana[51], 9 admitted stealing from a store within the past year, 24 admitted to lying to their parents about something significant, 18 admitted to cheating on a test during the last year, and 28 out of 30 are satisfied with their personal ethics and character[52].

Tossing your children into this student culture would be like tossing them into a lions' den. Only a miracle could save them.

Principle#5: A Biblical Education is Relational. (Deuteronomy 6: 5 – 7)

The public schools do exactly what they were designed to do. They were designed to separate children from their parents in order mold and shape them into

---

[49] Centers for Disease Control and Prevention (CDC)(2009)
[50] Gallup's National Values and Beliefs Survey (2007)
[51] The Partnership at Drugfree.org and MetLife Foundation (2011)
[52] Josephson Institute of Ethics (2010)

their image; indoctrinating them with their liberal, humanistic, morally relativistic beliefs. State curriculums, the media, and peer groups have replaced the parent's role as their children's primary influence. This has greatly contributed to the disintegration of the family and the weakening of the church. They steal the hearts and minds of our children while allowing their bodies to return home to eat and sleep. Rousseau, Dewey, and Marx would be very pleased.

Principle#6: Biblical Content.

The content of a Biblical education must be Gospel centered (Romans 1: 16) and saturated with the fear of the LORD (Proverbs 1: 7, Proverbs 9: 10), focused on the centrality of the Word of God (2 Timothy 3: 14 – 17), imparting a purely Biblical worldview (1Timothy 6: 20, 1 Corinthians 3: 18 – 20, Romans 12: 2), and instructing students in apologetics (1 Peter 3: 15, 2 Corinthians 10: 3 – 6), evangelism (Ephesians 4: 11 – 16), Biblical family roles (Ephesians 5: 23 – 6: 4), prayer (1 Thessalonians 5: 16 – 18), Bible study (Matthew 4: 4), scripture memorization (Psalm 119: 9 – 12), Christian service (1 Peter 4: 9 – 11), involvement in a local church (Hebrews 10: 24 – 25), and career training (1Timothy 5: 8, 2 Thessalonians 3: 10). This is the opposite of what is found in the public schools.

The idea that the public school curriculum is religiously neutral is a lie. The public schools deliberately indoctrinate children into a Jesus hating, morally relativistic, secular humanist worldview that is at war with Biblical Christianity. Evolution based science classes discredit the reliability of the Bible and get rid of God as Creator. The result of this is moral relativism. This is where human beings are left to be sovereign over their own lives, free to sin to their hearts content. History classes get rid of God as Sovereign King and demonize Christianity. English classes continue the assault by reinforcing the morally relativistic worldview through the literature they assign their students to read. In addition, through the deconstructionalist view of textual interpretation, they teach students that there is no objective way to interpret a text. This leads many to commit the hermeneutical error of isogesis when they read the Bible. In addition, the psychology based counselors and school programs churn out many students that end up with an artificially inflated self-esteem, a sense of entitlement, and an aversion to taking responsibility for their actions. These are individuals who believe that they are good people that deserve to go to heaven regardless of the evidence to the contrary.

If that wasn't enough, the public schools encourage the breaking of each and every one of the Ten Commandments through the morally relativistic worldview that they impart to their students on a daily basis. The public school curriculum systematically sabotages every element of the gospel and has led millions of children down the broad road to spiritual destruction.

Conclusion

By choosing to send our children t schools we are violating 6 clear Biblical co_____ and principles. We are cursing our children by giving them the exact opposite of what Psalm 1 prescribes. We are trading the law of the LORD for the doctrines of demons. We are knowingly placing them under the counsel of the wicked and making them stand in the way of sinners. The only possible result of our foolishness is that many of our children will end up sitting in the seat of mockers.

A whopping 89%[53] of children from Christian homes are placed in the public schools for their education. An astounding 70%[54] - 88%[55] of those children are leaving the visible church by the end of their freshman year in college. The most frustrating thing about this situation is that few in the church today are talking about this phenomenon, let alone speaking out against it. The public schools are truly the elephant in the room.

To our shame, the secular humanists know the true purpose of the public schools more than most Christians:

"I am convinced that the battle for humankind's future must be waged and won in the public school classroom by teachers who correctly perceive their role as the proselytizers of a new faith: a religion of humanity that recognizes and respects the spark of what theologians call divinity in every human being. These

---

[53] Nehemiah Institute (1988 – 2006) and Britt Beemer's America's Research Group's national survey (2006)
[54] LifeWay Research Survey (2007)
[55] Southern Baptist Council on the Family (2002)

...achers must embody the same selfless dedication as the most rabid fundamentalist preachers, for they will be ministers of another sort, utilizing a classroom instead of a pulpit to convey humanist values in whatever subject they teach, regardless of the educational level—preschool day care or large state university. The classroom must and will become an arena of conflict between the old and the new—the rotting corpse of Christianity, together with all its adjacent evils and misery, and the new faith of humanism."
(John Dunphy, A Religion for a New Age, Humanist, Jan.-Feb. 1983, p. 26)

"Education is the most powerful ally of Humanism, and every American public school is a school of Humanism. What can the theistic Sunday Schools, meeting for an hour once a week, and teaching only a fraction of the children do to stem the tide of a five-day program of Humanistic teaching?"
~Charles Francis Potter

It is obvious that the public schools are a devastating weapon intentionally designed by our enemies to destroy our children, our families, and our churches. With less than 1 percent of all Americans between the ages of 18 and 23 having a Biblical worldview[56] and with the fastest growing "religious group" in America being made up of people with no religion at all, with 13 million in that group identifying themselves as either atheists or

---

[56] Barna Group's nationwide survey (2009)

agnostics[57], it is safe to say that the public schools have been doing a great job of fulfilling their intended purpose.

After more than a decade of teaching in a public high school, seeing first-hand the spiritual carnage of public education, I feel like a fireman who has just come from the burning building that is the public schools with the smell of smoke still on my clothes. Seeing the destruction of our children, I can't help but scream, "Get your children out! The building is on fire, and many of your children are being burned alive!! GET YOUR CHILDREN OUT!!!"

If you won't listen to me, at least listen to Martin Luther when he said the following about the schools of his day:

"I advise no one to place his child where the Scriptures do not reign paramount. Every institution in which men are not increasingly occupied with the Word of God must become corrupt ... I am much afraid that schools will prove to be the great gates of hell unless they diligently labor in explaining the Holy Scriptures, engraving them in the hearts of youth."
~Martin Luther

---

[57] Pew Forum on Religion and Public Life survey (October, 2012)

CHAPTER NINE:
Countering the Salt and Light Argument

Even after people find out that the public schools violate all 6 commands and principles that make up a Biblical education, encourage the breaking of the Ten Commandments, and systematically sabotage the message of the gospel, there will still be some that will continue to bring up what I call the "Salt and Light" argument. This is the argument where people use the Great Commission as justification to violate the 6 clear Biblical commands and principles of a Biblical education in order to place their children in the public schools.

Many of the people who use this argument have godly intentions. They are committed to fulfilling the Great Commission for the glory of God and the salvation of men. They have applied God's law and the gospel of Jesus Christ to their own lives and have found out just how much they have been forgiven, and as a result, they have an overwhelming passion to love God with all their heart, soul, mind, and strength, and to love their neighbors as themselves (Mark 12: 30). These are people who have a holy obsession to preach the gospel to every creature (Mark16: 15). As a result, they look at the public schools as an unreached people group within a restricted country. And since students are the only people who have open access to preach the gospel in the public schools, it seems logical for these individuals to be advocates for the sending of children from Christian homes as missionaries to the public schools. On the surface this may sound reasonable and I whole heartedly share their gospel centered motivation, but there is a problem with this line of reasoning. It ignores many significant Biblical objections that make it clear that Christians should never send their children as missionaries to the public schools.

Biblical Objection #1: Children are easily corrupted.

The nature of children make them vulnerable to corruption (Proverbs 22: 15a and Ephesians 4: 14 – 15). Considering the toxic nature of the public school environment, even truly born again children are ill suited for this kind of missionary work.

Biblical Objection#2: Many of our children are false converts.

I am sure that we can all agree that the Great Commission was given to born again believers to accomplish. As a result, we can also agree that the first qualification of a missionary is their born again status. The problem is that it is obvious that 70%[58] – 88%[59] of

---

[58] LifeWay Research Survey (2007)

children from Christian homes that were sent to the public schools as "missionaries" were never born again Christians to begin with. They either never claimed to have saving faith or they were false converts. As 1 John 2: 19 says:

> *"They went out from us, but they were not of us; for if they had been of us, they would have continued with us. But they went out, that it might become plain that they all are not of us."*
> *(1John 2: 19)(Emphasis added)*

This is a big problem for the "salt and light" argument. How can these children be the salt and light in the public schools when God has not yet regenerated their hearts and lead them to repentance and faith? This is obviously a rhetorical question. The fact is that more than 7 out of every 10 children that we send into the spiritual battlefield that is the public schools are dead men walking. They are spiritually dead, and as a result, don't have the armor of God or the sword of the Spirit (Ephesians 6: 10 – 20). Unless God decides to have mercy and save some in spite of our totally incompetent tactical error, their end is inevitable. They will enter the battlefield as cannon fodder, unarmed and unprotected. They will be slaughtered.

This massacre has been happening and will continue to happen if we don't do something about it for two reasons. One, God never meant for children from

---

[59] Southern Baptist Council on the Family (2002)

Christian homes to be sent to the secular humanistic public schools for indoctrination; and two, many pastors have dropped the ball when it comes to preaching the gospel of Jesus Christ and teaching their congregations about the reality of true and false conversion.

Why did these false converts believe that they were born again Christians in the first place? There are many possible reasons. It could be that they were taught that Jesus died on the cross to give them prosperity or to meet their felt needs. It could be that they were taught that having an emotional experience at church followed by asking Jesus into their hearts would actually save them. It could be that they were baptized during early childhood and given false assurance of their salvation by their parents or pastors even though they never produced the fruit of repentance. It could be that since they were never commanded to repent of their sins, they believed that they could continue to love their sin and claim Jesus as their Savior at the same time. I could go on and on about the many perversions of the gospel that our American Christian culture has produced, but I'm sure you get my point. The church needs to hear the truth.

Pastors, if we were to succeed in sparking a mass exodus from the public schools, and every single child in your congregation were either sent to a Christian school or home schooled, we would still fail at preventing the loss of the next generation if you do not preach on every essential element that is needed to understand the true gospel of Jesus Christ and teach your flock about the reality of true and false conversion. Since this is such an important issue, bear with me as I present to you a message that I would preach to all who would listen:

Salvation, Sanctification, Glorification, and the Reality of True and False Conversion:

Imagine a giant room. On one side you have a trough filled with the most disgusting, rotten slop on the planet and on the other side you have a gourmet table with the most amazing food on the planet. What would happen if you let a pig loose into the room? Where would he go? He would go directly to the slop. It is in his nature to love slop. He has no idea how disgusting the slop is. He would dive into the slop, gorge himself on it, and wallow in it. He would have a pig party. The bad news is that this pig is you and I in our sin. It is in our nature to love sin. We have no idea how disgusting sin really is. But if God regenerates our hearts and makes us born again, it would be like God snapping His fingers and changing that pig into a human being in the middle of eating that slop. How do you think that human being would feel? Remember, he would be sitting there naked in the slop covered with filth, with his mouth full of slop. The first thing that he would probably do is vomit. He would feel absolutely wretched over what he had been eating. He would be overcome with shame. And if it were me, he would be filled with self-hatred for being the type of person that loved to eat rotten slop. And he would be desperate for someone to clean him.

This is the only time that Jesus comes to save anyone.

As Jesus said, Jesus came to save sinners, people who know how hopelessly wretched they are in their sins and know the depths of God's judgment that they deserve. He did not come to save those who think they are righteous but to call sinners to repentance and faith in Him. (Matthew 9: 12 – 14, Mark 2: 16 - 18, Luke 5: 31 – 33) But when He comes, He comes, and with Him a new life in Him through His resurrection!!! (Romans 6: 5 – 11) He lovingly washes you clean and makes you as white as snow (Isaiah 64: 6). He covers your shameful nakedness with His white robe of righteousness, the righteousness that He merited for you (Romans 5:17). God then fills you with His Holy Spirit (John 14: 23), adopts you as His child (Galatians 4: 4 – 7), and places you at the gourmet table to eat the good food of God. This all happens at the moment of salvation.

At this point, you are a true born again believer who has been made alive by the Holy Spirit and given a new heart (Ezekiel 36: 25 – 27). You have gone from loving sin and hating God to loving God and hating sin. At this point, you love Jesus more than anything in the universe including your own life because of the infinite love and mercy that Jesus has shown you by suffering the wrath of God that you deserved for your sins on the cross. As a result of your love for Jesus, you commit yourself to wage war against every sin that is in your life because it put your precious Jesus on the cross. This is the beginning of the process of sanctification.

Sanctification begins at the moment of salvation and ends when you see God face to face. During this period of time, God renews your mind with His Word and progressively takes sin after sin out of your life. At the same time, it is also a period when you are still in the flesh and as a result, still tempted by sin. But every time you go back to the slop and take a bite (sin), you will immediately vomit and return to the good table because God is your Father and He disciplines His children (Hebrews 12: 5 – 11). The next time you go to the slop and take a bite, you vomit again, and again you go back to the good table. Eventually, the smell alone will make you sick and you stop going back to that particular slop all together. This happens time and time again during the process of sanctification until you see God face to face. That is when He glorifies you and finishes the job of transforming you into the image of His Son so you can be with Him forever in heaven. (Romans 8: 29)

On the other hand, there are some people who on the surface look like they belong to the family of God and sit at the good table, but in reality, they are fake Christians. When no one is looking, they sneak over to the slop. But instead of just taking a bite, getting sick, and then returning to the good table, they dive right in and gorge themselves on that disgusting slop. As long as they don't get caught, they continue to return to the slop in order to indulge in their favorite sins. God's discipline is obviously not in their lives. This in itself is a strong indication that they are false converts.

"And have you forgotten the exhortation that addresses you as sons? 'My son, do not regard lightly the discipline

> *of the Lord, nor be weary when reproved by Him. <u>For the Lord disciplines the one He loves, and chastises every son whom He receives.</u>' It is for discipline that you have to endure. God is treating you as sons. For what son is there whom his father does not discipline? <u>If you are left without discipline, in which all have participated, then you are illegitimate children and not sons.</u>"*
> *(Hebrews 12: 5 – 8)(Emphasis added)*

God is not a negligent Father. Therefore, if God's discipline is not in a person's life, then that person is not a child of God. And if a person is not a child of God, then that person is a liar who is still spiritually dead in their trespasses and sins, still a slave to sin, and of the devil.

> *"This is the message we have heard from Him and proclaim to you, that God is light, and in Him is no darkness at all. <u>If we say we have fellowship with Him while we walk in darkness, we lie and do not practice the truth.</u>" (1 John 1: 5 – 6)(Emphasis added)*

> *"<u>Whoever makes a practice of sinning is of the devil</u>, for the devil has been sinning from the beginning. The reason the Son of God appeared was to destroy the works of the devil. <u>No one born of God makes a practice of sinning,</u> for God's seed abides in him, and he cannot keep on sinning because he has been born of God."*
> *(1 John 3: 8 – 9)(Emphasis added)*

Do these passages suggest that true born again Christians don't sin? Absolutely not!

> *"But if we walk in the light, as He is in the light, we have fellowship with one another, and the blood of Jesus His Son cleanses us from all sin. <u>If we say we have no sin, we deceive ourselves, and the truth is not in us. If we confess our sins, He is faithful and just to forgive us our sins and to cleanse us from all unrighteousness.</u> If we say we have not sinned, we make Him a liar, and His word is not in us." (1John 1: 7 – 10)(Emphasis added)*

What these passages do suggest is that if you are not actively at war with your sin with the help of the Holy Spirit, but instead love your sin and make a practice of sinning, then you are of the devil. Regeneration by the Holy Spirit has not taken place. Your faith is dead (James 2: 17). As a result, you are not a child of God. You are a child of wrath (Ephesians 2: 3).

Do not be deceived. You cannot love sin and love Jesus at the same time. You cannot serve two masters. You must hate one and love the Other (Matthew 6: 24, Luke 16: 13).

If you are one of these people, you may be able to fool the people at church, but you will never be able fool Jesus.

Jesus spoke clearly regarding how He would respond to fake Christians on Judgment Day:

> *"Not everyone who says to me, 'Lord, Lord,' will enter the kingdom of heaven, but the one who does the will of my Father who is in heaven. On that day many will say to me, 'Lord, Lord, did we not prophesy in your name, and cast out demons in your name, and do many mighty works in your name?' And then will I declare to them, 'I never knew you; depart from Me, you workers of lawlessness.'" (Matthew 7: 21 – 23)*

"I never knew you". I cannot imagine the depths of hopelessness and despair that I would feel if I were to hear those words from Jesus Christ Himself.

It is clear from this passage that the people that Jesus is referring to are people who are devout church goers and even seem to be doing mighty works for God, but are not true born again Christians. On the surface they may have seemed to be faithful servants of Christ who proclaimed His Name, but Jesus NEVER knew them. The Holy Spirit never regenerated their hearts. As a result, they continued to love sin and practice lawlessness. And their end is outer darkness where there will be weeping and gnashing of teeth (Matthew 8: 12, 22: 13, 25: 30) and the lake of fire where

> *"he also will drink the wine of God's wrath, poured full strength into the cup of His anger, and he will be tormented with fire and sulfur in the presence of the holy angels and in the presence of the Lamb. And the smoke of their torment goes up forever and ever, and they have no rest, day or night," (Revelation 14: 10 – 11b)*

> *"Examine yourselves, to see whether you are in the faith. Test yourselves. Or do you not realize this about yourselves, that Jesus Christ is in you?—unless indeed you fail to meet the test!" (2 Corinthians 13: 5)*

My heart breaks for you. For you could be members of my own family. Please listen to me. Jesus loved you so much that He suffered the wrath of God that you deserved for your sins. He died to save your eternal soul. Cry out to God. Throw yourselves at His mercy. Confess your sins to Him and beg Him to forgive you. Repent of your sins and trust in Jesus as your Lord and Savior. Then He will save you and transform you into someone who could be the salt and the light in this dark world.

Jesus described the regenerated heart, the renewed mind, and the transformed life of a true born again Christian in the Beatitudes at the beginning of Jesus' Sermon on the Mount.

> *"Seeing the crowds, He went up on the mountain, and when He sat down, His disciples came to Him. And He opened His mouth and taught them, saying: "Blessed are the poor in spirit, for theirs is the kingdom of heaven." (Matthew 5:1-3)*

A true child of God is poor in spirit. He knows that all of his good works are filthy rags (Isaiah 64:6). He knows he has no righteousness of his own (Romans 3: 10). In his heart, he understands that all he has earned for himself in this life is an eternity in hell. In the end, he joyfully accepts and is eternally grateful that for all of eternity he will merely be an example of God's incredible mercy and grace; while Jesus receives all of the credit, honor, and glory for his salvation.

> *"Blessed are those who mourn, for they shall be comforted." (Matthew 5: 4)*

A true child of God has a deep godly sorrow over his sin. He doesn't have worldly sorrow, which is only concerned with the consequences of sin. On the contrary, the primary cause of his mourning is his offense against Almighty God. This godly sorrow led the true child of God to genuine repentance and saving faith in his Lord and Savior.

> *"For godly sorrow produces repentance leading to salvation, not to be regretted; but the sorrow of the world produces death." (2 Corinthians 7: 10)*

> *"Blessed are the meek, for they shall inherit the earth." (Matthew 5: 5)*

A true child of God is meek towards God. He has been given a teachable spirit, one who craves to have his mind renewed and life reformed by the Word of God. He is ready and willing to toss in the garbage every single thought and opinion that is contrary to the Word of God, and to trust and obey God's Word alone. His heart's desire is to live by His Word.

> *"Blessed are those who hunger and thirst for righteousness, for they shall be satisfied." (Matthew 5: 6)*

A true child of God has had his heart regenerated (Titus 3: 5). He has been set free from being a slave to sin and has become a slave to righteousness (Romans 6: 15 – 23). In response to the love that God has shown him, he strives with all of his heart, soul, mind, and strength with the help of the Holy Spirit, to put to death the sin that is in his flesh (Romans 8: 13, Colossians 3: 5) and to live his life for the glory of God (1 Corinthians 10: 31).

> *"Blessed are the merciful, for they shall receive mercy." (Matthew 5: 7)*

A true child of God realizes how much he has been forgiven and as a result, loves much in return (Luke 7: 36 – 47). Mercy is something that pours forth out of the heart of a true child of God.

> *"Blessed are the pure in heart, for they shall see God." (Matthew 5: 8)*

A true child of God has been washed clean by the blood of the Lamb. He is no longer under any condemnation (Romans 8: 1). God Himself has given him a new heart, filled him with His Spirit, and made him pure in heart with a desire to seek after holiness. God describes how He would do this in a prophesy that He gave the prophet Ezekiel concerning the new covenant.

> *"I will sprinkle clean water on you, and you shall be clean from all your uncleannesses, and from all your idols I will cleanse you. And I will give you a new heart, and a new spirit I will put within you. And I will remove the heart of stone from your flesh and give you a heart of flesh. And I will put my Spirit within you, and cause you to walk in my statutes and be careful to obey my rules."*
> *(Ezekiel 36: 25 – 27)*

God utterly transforms His children and causes their hearts to seek after holiness, because without holiness no one will see the Lord (Hebrews 12:14); but those who are pure in heart will see God.

> *"Blessed are the peacemakers, for they shall be called sons of God." (Matthew 5:9)*

A true child of God has been made an ambassador of God, charged with delivering God's message of reconciliation to the world (2 Corinthians 5: 17 – 20). His heart's desire is to see His King, the Lord Jesus Christ, receive the reward of His suffering and to see his neighbor saved from the fires of hell that he himself deserved for his sins. His holy obsession is to reconcile rebellious people to the God that he loves, to broker peace between God and men. When he sees a man running toward the edge of a cliff about to dive headlong into the lake of fire, he is compelled by his love for God and his neighbor to stand in his way. He is driven to do this with great resolve thinking, "if this man is determined to dive off this cliff, he will have to get through me first." This is the heart of a peacemaker.

> *"Blessed are those who are persecuted for righteousness' sake, for theirs is the kingdom of heaven.*
> *"Blessed are you when others revile you and persecute you and utter all kinds of evil against you falsely on my account. Rejoice and be glad, for your reward is great in heaven, for so they persecuted the prophets who were before you." (Matthew 5: 10 – 12)*

A true child of God loves God more than his own life. He is willing to deny himself, pick up his cross, and follow Jesus no matter how horrible the persecution. He is willing to lose his job, his home, his friends, his family, his reputation, his health, and even his own life for the sake of Jesus Christ and His gospel.

> As Jesus said, *"If anyone would come after Me, let him deny himself and take up his cross and follow Me. For whoever would save his life will lose it, but whoever loses his life for My sake and the gospel's will save it." (Mark 8: 34b – 35)*

Ultimately, you don't have to be perfect in each of these characteristics to be a true child of God since the

Word of God tells us that true born again Christians will continue to be imperfect until this life is over or until Jesus returns. That is when God will glorify us and make us into the perfect image of His Son.

On the other hand, if you don't see yourself described in the Beatitudes, or don't see evidence that the Holy Spirit is progressively growing you in these areas, then I plead with you:

Turn to God. Go to the cross. Stop loving your sin. Stop trusting your good works. Turn away from them and embrace our Lord Jesus. Repent of your sins and have faith in Him as your Savior and Lord, and He will save you.

> *"Come now, let us reason together, says the LORD:*
> *though your sins are like scarlet,*
> *they shall be as white as snow;*
> *though they are red like crimson,*
> *they shall become like wool." (Isaiah 1: 18)*

> *"For God so loved the world, that He gave His only Son, that whoever believes in Him should not perish but have eternal life." (John 3: 16)*

In the end, we must preach this message to all who would listen, take our children out of the public schools, and provide them with a purely Biblical education. This is the only way we are going to have any hope of ending the generational crisis that we find ourselves in.

Biblical Objection # 3: God's will is perfect.

Even if you were certain that your child was a born again Christian and you were able to compensate for your child's natural spiritual vulnerability through intensive discipleship, the Word of God is clear that we should never throw our children into a pit of vipers such as the public schools. Even for a goal as noble as the Great Commission, public education is not an option because it violates all 6 Biblical commands and principles that make up a Biblical education. Since this is the case, we can trust that God has predetermined other means to save the elect from the public schools.

God's will is perfect.

"Do not be conformed to this world, but be transformed by the renewal of your mind, that by testing you may discern what is the <u>will of God</u>, what is good and acceptable and <u>perfect</u>." (Romans 12: 2)

God would never have us violate His perfect will in one area in order to fulfill it in another. In God's moral economy, the ends never justify the means. Being willing to break God's commands and principles for a Biblical education for the sake of trying to fulfill the Great Commission is to declare that God's will is not perfect. This blasphemous attitude places our wisdom as superior to God's, and is the epitome of arrogance, pride, and self-worship. The heart of this sin is the same as Adam's sin that resulted in the Fall of Man. *"Pride goes before destruction, and a haughty spirit before a fall." (Proverbs 16: 18)* and fallen we have. I'm begging you. Please do not sacrifice your children on the altar of ministry. Take your children out of the public schools. It is God's good, acceptable, and perfect will.

Real Life Testimony

By now, I am sure you understand that this issue is not hypothetical or theoretical in nature. This issue is about real children from Christian homes who are wrongly sent as cannon fodder to the spiritual battlefield that is the public schools in the name of the Great Commission. The fact is our tactical error is causing real pain to real families and dishonor to our Lord Jesus Christ.

The following is a testimony of a father who came to the conclusion that the "salt and light" argument is not valid the hard way, but thankfully just in time. This testimony was originally posted on the IndoctriNation Blog[60] by Joaquin Fernandez, co-producer of the award-winning documentary *"IndoctriNation: Public Schools and the Decline of Christianity in America."*[61]

"I am a homeschooling father of seven who recently viewed *IndoctriNation* with my family; it truly confirmed our experience. We have not always homeschooled our kids, even though we originally set out to do so. My wife

---

[60] http://blog.indoctrinationmovie.com/
[61] http://www.indoctrinationmovie.com/

and I homeschooled our children until 2006, the year we placed them in public schools. My oldest daughter's first grade in public school was 10th; my youngest entered kindergarten the following year. We thought we had legitimate reasons for our decision, and thought we could counter any problematic information they received along the way. We were naïve.

We decided to public school our kids after we bought a new house, having rented for years. The new home fell within a very well-respected school district, one whose schools ranked among the top 200 nationwide, so we felt very good about the local schools' academics. However, I think the greatest factor driving our decision to place our kids in public school was pressure to evangelize. I worked a full time secular job, but also served a local church as a credentialed part-time Associate Pastor. As a church, we strongly promoted relationship-based evangelism, and encouraged people to intentionally build relationships with non-believers to whom they could share their faith. We called it getting out of the 'church bubble.' My kids had grown up with faith in Christ, and I was confident in their spiritual preparation and resilience, and I expected them to weather the changes without any problem.

For their part, my kids were excited to try public school. It never occurred to me how iconic those yellow school buses are until watching *IndoctriNation*, but until buying our house, we lived right on our neighborhood's school bus stop. Public school must have seemed marvelously fun to my kids, seeing all those other neighborhood children getting off their buses and skipping home every afternoon, artwork and projects flapping in the wind.

And to tell the truth, there was a certain amount of selfish relief my wife and I felt after having made our decision. Our budget was very tight, and we were looking forward to not having the expenses of homeschooling our six-going-on-seven kids. We expected the time requirements devoted toward our kid's education to decrease as we moved from driving to supporting roles. And one child in particular was less interested in learning than the others (translate: lazy!), and we expected to bear less opposition from him in the process, too.

All in all, we were wrong... wrong... wrong... and... wrong.

First off, public school is not 'free,' at least not where we live. Our school district had tons of hidden costs for field trips, special materials, PTA functions, social events, and buying extra classroom pens, pencils, snacks, and facial tissue. There was even an increase in my kids' overall lunch costs. We easily spent twice as much on school-related expenses after public-schooling than we ever did homeschooling.

Second, I would say we saw absolutely no decrease in our time commitments. Changing to public school simply back-loaded our day, meaning we spent evenings helping the kids with their learning instead of our previous homeschooling routine of mornings and afternoons.

Third, my child who leaned toward laziness actually was harder to 'encourage' toward academic success in public school. Once he became one of thirty students, in one of several classes for each given teacher, he had much less accountability. Plus, there is an unavoidable disconnect of information flowing between a teacher and the parent in that circumstance. His teachers and I emailed frequently; however, there are limitations regarding what I could reasonably expect from his teachers' attention given that he became one of so many students.

Finally, what about my kids being salt and light? The basic idea that children should be lights in the world is a legitimate, Biblical concept. I support my kids being salt and light. However, I've come to the conclusion that I misapplied Biblical instruction meant for adult believers to children who shouldn't be expected to function at the same level of spiritual hardiness that God expects from adults. I think a better application for my kids being salt and light is for them to do so under the protection of our family.

Here is a few of the experiences we had through four years of public schooling, a choice that left its mark on each one of my kids.

My oldest daughter gravitated toward "scene" and "thug" culture, and struggled with making healthy social choices. As with all my kids, she and I would talk at length about her school experiences, and she seemed to voice agreement with my guidance, but her actions away from home were inconsistent with our discussions. At one point, she became "best friends" with another teen girl who attended church but who clearly had one foot placed firmly in both faith and secular worlds; this other girl's friendly but non-Christian mother seemed to make it a "trio" of girls hanging out. There came a time when this other mother had a greater voice with my daughter than my wife and I, simply because she was pleasant and sociable, and her worldly counsel was more to my daughter's liking.

My second daughter entered public school in ninth grade. She was an academic whiz, one of our state's top five percent. Public school helped her become very pro-gay and a Marxist pro-feminist. No exaggeration. She stopped going to church and in the resultant conflict, she actually had teachers helping her find an apartment of her own.

My third child was the less motivated one. As I mentioned, he was much less accountable, and much more able to fly under the radar. He experimented with cheating and theft, the opportunity for which he never would have had if we continued homeschooling him. I understand the root of these behaviors was rebellion, which would have manifested itself at home, too. However, I think he would have arrived at repentance more quickly if he had a greater level of accountability.

My middle son became incredibly popular in public school, and started thoroughly integrating into pop culture, gravitating to the skateboarder persona. His popularity gave him pressure to understate his Christianity, which came to something of a crisis when one of the kids he knew at school died in an accident, and my son dealt with guilt over never telling the boy about Christ. However, his environment was hostile to Christianity. At one point, my son was sent to detention because he referred to a glass of H_2O in science class as "Jesus Juice." Before getting remanded to detention, he had to sit in a class of his peers as the teacher ranted at him regarding how the classroom was no place for faith, and that our country was founded on principles of separation of church and state. The dialogue as related to me later by my son suggested the teacher had complete ignorance of the true philosophical origins of our country.

My next daughter is an average student, and even struggles some, especially with Math. She was pretty well overlooked in public school. In every school, there is at least one teacher that everyone recognizes as the bad one that no one wants for their children, and that person was my daughter's math teacher. This woman would shout at the kids, become angry when they did not grasp a concept, or would ignore requests for assistance because she didn't have time; consequently, my daughter was stagnant in learning Math. Socially, my daughter's personality is soft-hearted and non-confrontational. Her public school experience included frequently suffering from the meanness and drama so often stereotyped among school girls, and she herself picked up some of her peers' tendencies toward manipulation and drama.

My second youngest was classified as "gifted;" however, schools teach to the average and so he spent a lot of time with nothing to do. He also had a bladder issue that made him have serious urgency to use the restroom without really much notice. We explained the issue with his teacher, who was sympathetic, and who told my son that he could dash out whenever he needed to. She was quite compassionate. However, my son didn't like the attention created by his bathroom needs, and so he often waited when he really should have run to the restroom. This waiting in fact made the issue worse, because it led to bladder spasms. The result was wet pants, more social attention, and greater hesitance on his part to just run to the bathroom when the urge struck. It was a vicious cycle of humiliation.

My youngest was also classified as gifted. As a result she, like her brother, spent substantial time with nothing to do. Like her older sister, we found her suffering because of social game-playing and little-girl drama. Her classroom discussions of fire danger and stranger danger led to years of general fearfulness, including frequent nightmares. She was unable to play in a room alone, or have her parents out of the house. Most of her teachers were kind and caring, but there was the occasional substitute teacher with horrid classroom management skills. My wife, who volunteered at the elementary school to be near our kids, happened by this daughter's classroom once when a sub was teaching, and overheard the sub yelling and threatening to duct-tape the kids' mouths shut if they weren't quiet. The sub was completely unable to control the kids, and right then my wife entered the classroom, removed my daughter, and excused her from school for the rest of the day, following a pointed discussion with the school's Principal. What if my wife had not been there?

In not one instance can I say that my kids were able to make a significant salt-and-light impact in their public schools, regardless of how popular they were. The truth is, in every case, their own faith and walk with Christ universally suffered from the experience. The Old Testament is filled with case studies of what happens when God's people surround themselves with a pagan culture; how was it that I expected something different for my kids whose faith was only developing?

The primary mandate I have for my children comes from Deuteronomy 6:7-9, which tells me to teach my children about their Lord, all day, every day, constantly, without ceasing. It's impossible for me to do that if my kids are receiving their education outside the home. This passage made me realize that my primary error lay in thinking of schooling simply as education. How I choose to school my kids, though, is really not at all about education, but about discipleship. Simply stated, when I put my kids in public school, I relinquished the greatest influence I have to disciple them, and I delegated that role to the teachers and students of the public school: I chose to have my kids discipled by Humanists.

We've had our kids back home now for two years, and have moved beyond most of the adverse effects caused by public schooling, but it's been hard work. Watching home videos recently was painful; we could all see the changes in our family during that time. My kids will tell you they dislike who they became and it unified my kids as pro-home-school. By the grace of God, we have been restored."[62]

---

[62] IndoctriNation Blog, April 19, 2012, http://blog.indoctrinationmovie.com/2012/04/19/a-fathers-testimony/

What Do We Do Now?

CHAPTER TEN:
Repent

Even after being informed about what the Bible says regarding public education and hearing the testimony of others, many Christian parents will continue to justify their decision to send their children to the public schools in a variety of ways. But no matter what excuse is given, by sending their children to the public schools, parents are sinning against God.

1. They have given up their God given responsibility to bring up their children in the discipline and instruction of the Lord.

2. Instead, they have yoked themselves with a God hating, demonic institution. In a spiritual way, they have unwittingly given their children to "Molech", and made them walk in the counsel of the wicked, stand in the way of sinners, and sit in the seat of scoffers.

3. These parents have ignored the Biblical warnings regarding the spiritually vulnerable nature of children and the fact that bad company truly does corrupt good character. In spite of these warnings, they have decided to throw their children into the defiling cesspool that is the public school student culture.

4. By sending their children to the public schools, whether they know it or not, they have directly endorsed the indoctrination of their children. Ultimately, in the name of education, they have trained their children to reject God and His Word. The fact that 70%[63] - 88%[64] of the children leave the visible church demonstrates the negative fulfillment of Proverbs 22: 6:

> *"Train up a child in the way he should go,*
> *Even when he is old he will not depart from it.*
> *(Proverbs 22: 6)*

The children have been trained up in post-modern, secular humanist schools; and as God's Word and common sense would predict, they have become post-moderns and secular humanists on the broad road to hell instead of Bible believing Christians.

5. In the end, Jesus has given a very stern warning to people who would deliberately place children in an environment where it is almost impossible not to sin.

---

[63] LifeWay Research Survey (2007)
[64] Southern Baptist Council on the Family (2002)

> *"but whoever causes one of these little ones who believe in me to sin, it would be better for him to have a great millstone fastened around his neck and to be drowned in the depth of the sea."* (Matthew 18: 6)

If you are one of these people, what does your flesh desire so much that would lead you to willfully rebel against God by sending your children to the public schools? Is it your pride? Have you been defending your decision so long that you can't allow yourself to admit that you were wrong? Do you think you know better than God when it comes to raising your children? Or do you think that God doesn't know how to accomplish the Great Commission without sending your children to the public schools? Do you really think you are wiser than God?

God says,

> *"For as the heavens are higher than the earth,*
> *so are My ways higher than your ways*
> *and My thoughts than your thoughts."* (Isaiah 55: 9)
>
> *"Oh, the depth of the riches and wisdom and knowledge of God! How unsearchable are His judgments and how inscrutable His ways!*
> *'For who has known the mind of the Lord, or who has been His counselor?'"* (Romans 11: 33 – 34)

God is sovereign, all powerful, all knowing, all wise, and God is love. God pours out His amazing love on His children in abundance. He has orchestrated every single detail of your life from the trials to the triumphs for your good and His glory. In the same way, He has prescribed for us in His Word the best way to live our lives. Any wisdom that we think we have on any subject, including the Great Commission and the education of our children, is foolishness compared to the wisdom of God. Your Father in Heaven loves you. You can trust Him.

*"Trust in the LORD with all your heart,
and do not lean on your own understanding.
In all your ways acknowledge Him,
and He will make straight your paths.
Be not wise in your own eyes;
fear the LORD, and turn away from evil."
(Proverbs 3: 5 – 7)*

Repent of your pride and humble yourself before the Lord, and He will lift you up.

*"But He gives more grace. Therefore He says "God resists the proud, but gives grace to the humble." Therefore submit to God. Resist the devil and he will flee from you. Draw near to God and He will draw near to you. Cleanse your hands, you sinners; and purify your hearts, you double-minded. Lament and mourn and weep! Let your laughter be turned to mourning and your joy to gloom. Humble yourselves in the sight of the Lord, and He will lift you up."
(James 4: 6 – 10) (NKJV)*

Are you choosing to not trust God because of your desire for earthly treasure? Is having a two income household more important than God and your children? Are you afraid that by providing a Biblical education for your children you won't have enough money to have the lifestyle that you desire?
God says,

> *"But those who desire to be rich fall into temptation, into a snare, into many senseless and harmful desires that plunge people into ruin and destruction. For the love of money is a root of all kinds of evils. It is through this craving that some have wandered away from faith and pierced themselves with many pangs." (1Timothy 6: 9 – 11)*

Please, do not be like the rich young ruler:

> *"The young man said to Him, "All these I have kept. What do I still lack?" Jesus said to him, "If you would be perfect, go, sell what you possess and give to the poor, and you will have treasure in heaven; and come, follow Me." When the young man heard this he went away sorrowful, for he had great possessions.*
> *And Jesus said to His disciples, "Truly, I say to you, only with difficulty will a rich person enter the kingdom of heaven. Again I tell you, it is easier for a camel to go through the eye of a needle than for a rich person to enter the kingdom of God."*
> *(Matthew 19: 20 – 24)*

Please listen to Jesus' warnings about money. According to God's Word, having money is not evil in of itself. Job and Abraham were both very rich, but at the same time both were still seen as righteous before God through faith. It is the love of money that is the problem. Financial resources can be a gift from God. The problem is that most rich people fall in love with their money and make an idol out of it. That is when they wander away from the faith, ignore the wisdom of God's word, and pierce themselves with many pangs. These are the people like the rich young ruler who choose their comfortable lifestyles over following Jesus. These are the people who are guilty of the sin of idolatry and won't enter the kingdom of God.

Refusing to give your children a Biblical education because of the lifestyle changes that it would bring is to love money and earthly comfort more than you love God and your children. This is idolatry, and if you do not repent, you and your family will suffer many pangs.

> *"Do not lay up for yourselves treasures on earth, where moth and rust destroy and where thieves break in and steal, but lay up for yourselves treasures in heaven, where neither moth nor rust destroys and where thieves do not break in and steal. For where your treasure is, there your heart will be also." (Matthew 6: 19 – 21)*

Be reasonable. See this issue through God's eyes. Earthly treasure is of no eternal value. It could be taken away from you in an instant. There could be a natural or economic disaster, or your life could simply end. Any way you look at it, earthly treasure quickly passes away. Throughout history, how many kings and empires have risen, fallen, and faded from memory?

> "For, "All people are like grass,
> and all their glory is like the flowers of the field;
> the grass withers and the flowers fall,
> but the word of the Lord endures forever."
> And this is the word that was preached to you."
> (1Peter 1: 24 – 25) (NIV)

On the other hand, fulfilling the Great Commission in your home by providing your children with a Biblical education will not only result in blessing your family for generations to come, but also in heavenly treasure. Choosing to obey God by providing a Biblical education for your children has great eternal value. Do not live for this world. Live for eternity!

Are you choosing to not trust God because you think that the time required to provide a Biblical education for your children will interfere with your pursuit of self-fulfillment or pleasure?"
God says,

> "And calling the crowd to Him with His disciples, He
> said to them, "If anyone would come after Me, let
> him deny himself and take up his cross and follow
> Me. For whoever would save his life will lose it, but

> *whoever loses his life for My sake and the gospel's will save it." (Mark 8: 34 – 35)*

This is your "martyrdom" moment. In this country, you will probably never have to face being murdered for your faith; but each time you come to a crossroads in your life where you are given the choice between living for yourself and giving up your selfish way of life for Jesus, you are faced with the same decision as a martyr. You can choose to save your selfish way of life by denying Jesus and His Word, or you can choose to deny yourself, pick up your cross and follow Him. Choose to provide a Biblical education for your children. Declare to the world that Jesus is Lord! In the end, anything that you would have accomplished living for yourself would have been worthless anyway.

"What are all the accomplishments of this world in comparison to the smallest act of obedience to Christ? The fulfillment of even the most minute Christian duty is a greater achievement than the climbing of Everest or the winning of the Nobel Prize. Even giving a cup of cold water in His name does not go without divine notice or eternal reward. Let us then, serve the Lord with all our hearts and every fiber of our strength. Why should we spend ourselves for temporal trinkets, when eternal glory is within our grasp? In the words of Elliot, 'He is no fool to give up that which he cannot keep, to gain that which he can never lose.'

Finally, what are the trophies of this age in

comparison to the souls of men? There are many things in this world that can be won by perseverance and sacrifice, but none of them are eternal. Gold metals and the accolades of men, houses, lands, and riches are quick to rot and rust. Those who seek them are on a fool's errand, but he who wins souls is wise. It has been said that there are only three things eternal – God, the Word of God, and the souls of men. Let us press hard to win them before it is too late."[65]

This is the call of the Great Commission; and as parents, the Great Commission begins with providing a Biblical education for our children no matter the cost.

Are you choosing to not trust God because you are afraid that you won't have enough money to provide a Biblical education for your children? Do you not trust that God will provide what you need to do His will? God says,

"Therefore I tell you, do not be anxious about your life, what you will eat or what you will drink, nor about your body, what you will put on. Is not life more than food, and the body more than clothing? Look at the birds of the air: they neither sow nor reap nor gather into barns, and yet your heavenly Father feeds them. Are you not of more value than they? And which of you by being anxious can add a single hour to his span of life? And why are you anxious about clothing? Consider the lilies

---

[65] Excerpt from Paul Washer, HeartCry Magazine, November-December 2009, p. 2

of the field, how they grow: they neither toil nor spin, yet I tell you, even Solomon in all his glory was not arrayed like one of these. But if God so clothes the grass of the field, which today is alive and tomorrow is thrown into the oven, will he not much more clothe you, O you of little faith? Therefore do not be anxious, saying, 'What shall we eat?' or 'What shall we drink?' or 'What shall we wear?' For the Gentiles seek after all these things, and your heavenly Father knows that you need them all. But seek first the kingdom of God and His righteousness, and all these things will be added to you."
(Matthew 6: 25 – 33)

Remember, the average American Christian is very rich compared to the majority of Christians around the world. Many of the things that we think we need are simply luxuries that most Christians live without. Many Christians around the world live in what we would consider to be tiny homes packed with multigenerational families in conditions that we would consider to be poverty. We have become accustomed to a certain level of comfort and luxury. We have become spoiled by the American way of life and we think that we couldn't bear to give any of it up. But the fact is that downsizing our house and budget, living with only one used family car, not going on expensive vacations, and cutting coupons to go grocery shopping are not very big sacrifices to make for the souls of our children and the glory of our God.

I know that the decision to provide a Biblical education for your children can be intimidating. You might have to sacrifice considerable money, time, and energy; and you might not think that you are up for the task; but God will provide what you need to fulfill the Great Commission in your own home. Through His church He will equip you for this ministry (Ephesians 4: 11 – 15). By His Spirit He will empower you for this ministry (Acts 1:8). And He Himself will be with you to fulfill this ministry (Matthew 28: 20). In addition, He has given you His Word, the standard of Truth itself to sanctify you (John 17: 17) and to fully equip you for every good work (2 Timothy 3: 16 – 17). God's Love is truly amazing!

If you haven't done so already, repent! Take your children out of the public schools and do whatever it takes to provide them with a Biblical education. Turn to God and seek His forgiveness.

"Let us then with confidence draw near to the throne of grace, that we may receive mercy and find grace to help in time of need." (Hebrews 4: 16)

"If we confess our sins, He is faithful and just to forgive us our sins and to cleanse us from all unrighteousness." (1 John 1: 9)

CHAPTER ELEVEN:
Reform: Applying the Commands and Principles of a Biblical Education

A true Christian's life is full of transformation. We don't need to be afraid to make radical changes in our lives as we continually seek to deny ourselves, pick up our cross, and follow our Lord Jesus! We must cry out to God and ask him to change our hearts and renew our minds in regards to how we can best raise our children for His glory.

As you grow in the knowledge and understanding of God's word and humble yourself before God with a truly repentant heart, you will be ready to walk by faith and not by sight. God will give you the courage and conviction to take your children out of the public schools and begin to give them a truly Biblical education built upon the strong foundation of God's Holy Word.

It is time to reclaim your children from the world, turn your back on the public schools and take responsibility for your children's education. It doesn't matter at this point whether you decide to send your children to a Christian school committed to teaching a purely Biblical worldview or to home-school them. Both choices could be pleasing to God if done in faith.

I have personally chosen to home-school my children because I believe it gives me the best opportunity to fulfill all 6 of the commands and principles of a Biblical education; but comparing and contrasting these two options is a topic for another book. Right now the important thing is to remove your children from the public school's indoctrination no matter what personal sacrifices you have to make. The inconvenience of either increasing your educational expenses by sending your children to a Christian school or downsizing your budget so your wife can stay home to home-school, pale in comparison to the eternal task of caring for the souls of your children.

The following section covers how to further apply the 6 commands and principles of a Biblical education regardless of whether you are planning on sending your children to a Christian school or home-school.

Principle#1: Education belongs to the family supported by the church, not to the state. [66]

Fathers and mothers, this is where you begin to fulfill the Great Commission. This is your primary missions' field. As parents, every other aspect of the Great Commission should flow from this essential ministry. The evangelism and discipleship of your children is one of the most important ministries that you will ever have.

---

[66] Exodus Mandate, "Education belongs to the family, supported by the church, and not to the state", July 17, 2012

In order to accomplish this, I would strongly suggest that you adopt the practice of daily family worship. This is a daily time where you read scripture or other devotional materials to your children, sing praises to God together, and pray together as a family. It could be as short as 20 minutes to as long as your family can handle.

The following are excerpts from an article called *The Greatest Untapped Evangelistic Opportunity Before the Modern Church* written by Scott Brown, pastor at Hope Baptist Church and director of the N.C.F.I.C. These excerpts will inspire and challenge you as you strive to fulfill the Great Commission in your home through the daily practice of family worship and the discipleship that occurs when a family lives life together.

"The Bible calls fathers to preach the gospel to their children every day, when they "sit in their house, when they walk by the way, when they lie down and when they rise up" (Deuteronomy 6:7). A father is to pass on the knowledge of God to the next generation. He is commanded to expose his children day by day to the greatness of God, the perfections of His ways, and the great stories that explain His nature and character. This kind of instruction gives children a true understanding of the gospel.

Consider the Evangelistic Impact of Faithful Fathers

Think of the evangelistic impact that we as fathers would have in our generation if we would only heed this command. Consider the example of the faithful father:

Daily, he praises God to his children with hundreds of words and practical principles. Day after day, he cries out to them, explaining the stories that glorify the kindnesses of God, His wrath toward sinners, and His vanquishing power over all things. In so doing, he reflects the heart of the Heavenly Father who cries out, "Today if you will hear His voice, do not harden your hearts as in the rebellion" (Hebrews 3:7-11).

In turn, his children observe their father as he personally delights in the Word and places himself under its wonderful teaching. They behold how good and mighty God is and how foolish it is to turn away from Him. They see how their daddy is comforted and confronted by it and is changed before their eyes.

Under this kind of loving and happy ministry, children hear the whole counsel of God from Genesis to Revelation. They see the flow of history from God's perspective. They hear of the great doctrines of the faith which have sustained humble people from one generation to the next. They observe the mighty hand of God working against all human odds. They see the beginning and the end of history and where they themselves stand in its stream. They know who wins the battle. They know that nothing can stand against the will of our Sovereign Lord."[67]

Wow! How I pray that God will enable me to be faithful in this ministry. Doing daily family worship with my wife and children is the most rewarding part of my

---

[67] Scott Brown, *"The Greatest Untapped Evangelistic Opportunity Before the Modern Church"*, http://www.christianpost.com

day. I make sure that nothing stands in the way of this special time with my family. The consistent practice of family worship regardless of how I feel has established a sense of security, love, and peace in my household. It is a time where we not only explore the great deeds and wisdom of our God by studying His Word and attempt to give Him the worship that He deserves; it is also a time where I bear my soul to my family. It is a time where I confess my sins to them, including apologizing to them for how I have sinned against them. It is a time where we pray for each other in the gospel centered atmosphere of forgiveness and love. I am fully convinced that the consistent practice of family worship has deepened and strengthened our relationship as a family before God. It is through this practice that I feel I can echo Joshua's words,

> *"But as for me and my house, we will serve the LORD."(Joshua 24: 15)*

Family worship was faithfully practiced by most of the heroes of church history. It was a common practice among Christians until its decline in the late 1800's. Eventually the practice of family worship almost became extinct until its recent resurrection in pockets of Christendom that are experiencing a modern day Biblical reformation. In order for this Biblical reformation to spread for the glory of God, fathers and mothers need to be awakened from their false view of modern "successful" parenting.

"Fathers often feel great about their involvement in their children's lives because, rather than defining faithful fathering by what Scripture prescribes, they define exemplary fatherhood as going to the kid's recitals and games and getting them into a good Sunday school or youth group.

In order to rescue this lost generation of children in Christian homes from hell, we must first help fathers understand what God has commanded and exhort them to embrace their responsibilities before the Lord. We must speak clearly of what God has mandated so that fathers do not miss the opportunity to touch the hearts of their sons and daughters with the message of the gospel...

Please pray that we as fathers would not miss the greatest untapped evangelistic opportunity before the church today. Let it be said of this generation of fathers that we did our part to fulfill the Great Commission. May we preach the fullness of the gospel to our households daily as the Bible commands, and give our children a thousand reasons to believe."[68]

For more information on the practice of family worship, I recommend the following books: *Family Worship, in the Bible, in History, and in Your Home* by Dr. Don Whitney from Southern Baptist Theological Seminary. And *Family Worship* by Dr. Joel R. Beeke (Ph.D. Westminster Theological Seminary, president and

---

[68] Scott Brown, *"The Greatest Untapped Evangelistic Opportunity Before the Modern Church"*, http://www.christianpost.com

professor of systematic theology and homiletics at Puritan Reformed Theological Seminary, pastor of the Heritage Netherlands Reformed Congregation in Grand Rapids, Michigan, and speaker at John Piper's Desiring God Conference for Pastors 2011.) In addition, I suggest that you take advantage of some of the resources available at www.ncfic.org.

Principle#2: Do not be unequally yoked with unbelievers. (2 Corinthians 6: 14 – 18)

And

Principle#3: Teachers must have a godly character because a student will become like his teacher. (Luke 6: 39 – 40, and Psalm 1)

The people that you partner with in the evangelism and discipleship of your children are very important. Your children can be richly blessed by the influence of godly qualified pastors/elders at your church and by the fellowship of born again Christians that are committed to a life of holiness and the teaching of a purely Biblical worldview. If there is an individual or organization that you are currently partnering with that does not meet these qualifications, distance yourself and your family from their influence. This could include old friends and members of your extended family. Don't get me wrong, you can continue to love, preach the gospel to, disciple, and minister to these people just as long as you don't allow them to influence your family regarding worldly philosophies and practices. This can be a difficult tightrope to walk but at all costs, do not be unequally yoked. The negative influence that they could have on your children could be catastrophic.

Principle#4: Bad company really does corrupt good character. (Proverbs 13: 20) (1 Corinthians 15: 33)

Just as with principles #2 and #3, it is incredibly important to choose your children's peers carefully. When selecting your children's peer group, I would suggest that you use the same criteria as in the last section with one alteration. It is safe to assume that most children do not become born again Christians at a young age. Even if they do, it is hard for a parent to be certain until they are a little older and are producing consistent fruit. With that being said, it will have to suffice to select your children's peer group from likeminded families that are committed to Biblical child training and teaching their children a purely Biblical worldview. These are the type of peer relationships that have a strong potential to develop into godly friendships that will bless your children for a lifetime.

Principle#5: A Biblical education is relational. (Deuteronomy 6: 5 – 7)

Our careers, social lives, church ministries, and daily

business often make little time for tying heart strings with our children. We have to make a commitment to reprioritize our busy schedules and place our relationship with our children as a top priority. Contrary to popular belief, occasional moments of quality time are not enough to win their hearts. We need to live life with our children and spend time personally engaging them at their level, expressing delight at being in their presence. They need to know that you value them more than anything else in your life except for your relationship with God and your spouse. Investing generous amounts of quality time with them is the only way to build these relationships.

Principle#6: Biblical content.

The arts are considered by many to be the philosophy classrooms of our society. All forms of entertainment (art, literature, music, TV, movies, video games etc…) are vehicles that passively transport philosophies and worldviews into the minds of those who partake of them. As we passively sit to watch, listen, or read for entertainment, we naturally let down our guard, get sucked into the emotions of the characters or the beat of the music, and unknowingly absorb attitudes, philosophies, and aspects of worldviews that we would normally reject. The arts, from Hollywood to the Beetles to Harry Potter, are one of the primary tools that Satan has used to corrupt our culture over the last century.

Since most of us have grown up immersed in this

media cesspool, we have been desensitized. It is only through the power of the Holy Spirit and the renewing of our minds by the Word of God that we have any hope of developing even the smallest level of discernment. As God sanctifies us, He continually grows us in our discernment.

Satan does not always do his evil works in obvious ways. Some movies, TV shows, music, and books are obviously blasphemous, while others may seem wholesome in comparison, but in reality, they can be just as spiritually deadly. Much of this "wholesome" entertainment actually teaches an extremely unbiblical worldview. To make matters worse, many secular humanistic ideas such as evolution, psychology and radical feminism have infiltrated even "Christian" media. We must be vigilant in developing discernment as we seek to critically analyze our entertainment choices through the lens of the Bible. We are responsible for everything that we set before the eyes and ears of our children.

Rat poison is 99% good food yet it is deadly to the rats who consume it. In the same way, a lie can be 99% truth and yet be deadly to our children's minds, hearts, and souls. It is imperative for us to teach our children to discern between truth and lies. It is our God given responsibility to protect them from the lies of Satan, the father of lies.

The following is an excerpt from an article called "How Do We Pick?" from keepersofthefaith.com. This article does a great job of addressing the problem of the lack discernment that is inherent in children when compared to adults, and the necessity of being vigilant as parents when it comes to choosing books for our children. The concepts presented in this article could just as easily be applied to all other forms of media that we choose to give our children.

"Children do not have the discernment of adults, and, being impressionable, they tend to be affected by nearly everything they read as if it were truth. Authors, on the other hand, often like to build credibility for their pet preferences and beliefs by embedding them into the actions of characters in a seemingly wholesome story line. The young reader, being swept up into an exciting story, will begin identifying with whatever they read without recognizing that they are literally developing attitudes as they read—attitudes on important life issues—attitudes being built and nourished in them by a stranger—even attitudes which their parents are diligently attempting to train them not to have.

Many surprising attitudes are planted silently in the minds of children while they read. Harmful error often becomes part of a child's belief system by such osmosis. This usually takes place during, and in spite of, simultaneous parental instruction to the contrary. Ideas absorbed instinctively by one's emotions will be difficult to displace by reason. These ideas are often not even known to the child who absorbed them (part of the child's reasoning process). If they are not known to the child, how can either the harmful ideas and the source of those ideas be known to the parents? Parents who have labored to rear godly children have often been surprised and devastated by the unexpected attitudes sometimes displayed by their children. They have also been dismayed at finding out the strength and depth of these feelings (without logic) harbored by their children. They wonder at how such ideas could have occurred. Many of these attitudes were often developed through reading — reading what were assumed to be acceptable authors."[69]

Ultimately we need to watch, listen, and read everything that we are going to put in front of our children, and then we need to throw out anything that contradicts the Word of God. This is the only way that we can be sure that we are not sabotaging our own efforts of imparting a purely Biblical worldview to our children. This task sounds impossible, but if we work together as the body of Christ, we can accomplish it.

Many of the books and other media that I grew up with were like Trojan Horses deliberately designed to deliver their deadly cargo into my mind. For example, some of my favorite school books when I was a child were children's books about dinosaurs. Now I open them up and I read, "Millions of years ago. Long before humans ever existed ..." and I realize that my indoctrination into secular humanistic thinking began before I was 5 years old. This was the beginning of a treacherous journey into worldly ideas, ideas that could have led to my destruction. I am still being set free by

---

[69] http://www.keepersofthefaith.com/category/HowDoWePick

God's Word from all of the destructive teaching that I was fed through my own unbiblical education. With God's help, I have chosen to do everything possible to guard the hearts and minds of my children from evil and guide them to the path that leads to life in Christ Jesus. I hope that you make the same choice and choose to take part in this education reformation.

> *"Finally, brothers, whatever is true, whatever is honorable, whatever is just, whatever is pure, whatever is lovely, whatever is commendable, if there is any excellence, if there is anything worthy of praise, think about these things." (Philippians 4: 8)*

CHAPTER TWELVE:
Revive

Repentance followed by reformation bathed in prayer to our God leads to revival. The following are some of the things God told Solomon after Solomon finished the construction of the temple regarding this principle:

> *"When I shut up the heavens so that there is no rain, or command the locust to devour the land, or send pestilence among My people, if My people who are called by My name humble themselves, and pray and seek My face and turn from their wicked ways, then I will hear from heaven and will forgive their sin and heal their land." (2 Chronicles 7: 13 – 14)*

Our land has been hit with a pestilence. 70%[70] – 88%[71] of our children are walking away from the visible church. We need to humble ourselves, pray, and seek the face of our God. We need to turn from the wicked practice of sending our children to the public schools, and pray that

---

[70] LifeWay Research Survey (2007)
[71] Southern Baptist Council on the Family (2002)

the Holy Spirit opens the eyes and convicts the hearts of those in the church that are still partaking of public education. We need to pray that they repent of this sin and join the education reformation for the glory of God and the salvation of our children. May God have mercy on us, heal our land, and bring revival to the church.

Q&A For Parents: Getting Started

I have written this section for people who are looking to jump straight into home-schooling. At first, deciding to home-school may sound very intimidating, and for good reason. It might require you to sacrifice in many areas and make fundamental changes in how you live your life. Thankfully, by the grace of God working through the home-schooling pioneers that came before us, there are many resources available today that make home-schooling a very doable option regardless of your educational background or academic abilities.

<u>Question#1</u>: How do I start to home-school?

<u>Answer</u>: Home-schooling is legal in all 50 states, but the procedure for getting started varies from state to state. To find out the exact procedure for getting started in your state as well as tips on every aspect of home-schooling, go to the following websites:

1. Home School Legal Defense Association:www.hslda.org

2. You Can Home School: www.youcanhomeschool.org

Question#2: Will my children get an inferior academic education if we home-school?

Answer: No.

A nationwide study by Dr. Brian Ray, an internationally recognized scholar and president of the non-profit National Home Education Research Institute (NHERI), provides a definitive answer to this question. "Drawing from 15 independent testing services, the *Progress Report 2009: Homeschool Academic Achievement and Demographics* included 11,739 homeschooled students from all 50 states who took three well-known tests—*California Achievement Test, Iowa Tests of Basic Skills*, and *Stanford Achievement Test* for the 2007–08 academic year. The *Progress Report* is the most comprehensive home-school academic study ever completed.

The Results

Overall the study showed significant advances in home-school academic achievement as well as revealing that issues such as student gender, parents' education level, and family income had little bearing on the results of homeschooled students.

National Average Percentile Scores

Subtest	Home-school	Public School
Reading	89	50
Language	84	50
Math	84	50
Science	86	50
Social Studies	84	50
Core[a]	88	50
Composite[b]	86	50

a. Core is a combination of Reading, Language, and Math.
b. Composite is a combination of all subtests that the student took on the test.

There was little difference between the results of homeschooled boys and girls on core scores.

Boys—87th percentile
Girls—88th percentile

Household income had little impact on the results of homeschooled students.

> **$34,999 or less**—85th percentile
> **$35,000–$49,999**—86th percentile
> **$50,000–$69,999**—86th percentile
> **$70,000 or more**—89th percentile

The education level of the parents made a noticeable difference, but the homeschooled children of non-college educated parents still scored in the 83rd percentile, which is well above the national average.

> **Neither parent has a college degree**—83rd percentile
> **One parent has a college degree**—86th percentile
> **Both parents have a college degree**—90th percentile

Whether either parent was a certified teacher did not matter.

> **Certified (i.e., either parent ever certified)**—87th percentile
> **Not certified (i.e., neither parent ever certified)**—88th percentile

Parental spending on home education made little difference.

> **Spent $600 or more on the student**—89th percentile
> **Spent under $600 on the student**—86th percentile...

In short, the results found in the new study are consistent with 25 years of research, which show that as a group homeschoolers consistently perform above average academically. The *Progress Report* also shows that, even as the numbers and diversity of homeschoolers have grown tremendously over the past 10 years, homeschoolers have actually increased the already sizeable gap in academic achievement between themselves and their public school counterparts-moving from about 30 percentile points higher in the Rudner study (1998) to 37 percentile points higher in the *Progress Report* (2009).

The achievement gaps that are well-documented in public school between boys and girls, parents with lower incomes, and parents with lower levels of education are not found among homeschoolers. While it is not possible to draw a definitive conclusion, it does appear from all the existing research that homeschooling equalizes every student upwards. Homeschoolers are actually achieving every day what the public schools claim are their goals—to narrow achievement gaps and to educate each child to a high level.

Of course, an education movement which consistently shows that children can be educated to a standard significantly above the average public school student at a fraction of the cost—the average spent by participants in the *Progress Report* was about $500 per child per year as opposed to the public school average of nearly $10,000 per child per year—will inevitably draw attention from the K-12 public education industry."[72]

The results are clear, even from an academic achievement standpoint the home-school environment created by loving, dedicated parents can't be beat.

Besides research studies, there are plenty of experts in higher education that testify to the day to day reality of these impressive results. For example, Jack A. Chambless, an economics professor at Valencia College, wrote an article on June 10, 2012 in the Orlando Sentinel called *"Is it time to think about home schooling your child?"* In this article, he made a strong case for homeschooling as the best academic option in America. The following are some excerpts from his article:

"For the past 21 years I have taught economics to more than 14,000 college students here in Central Florida.

During that time I have made a concerted effort to glean information from my Valencia students as to their educational background preceding their arrival in college.

Drawing from a sample size this large multiplied by two decades multiplied by hundreds of thousands of test answers has put me in a good position to offer the following advice to any reader of this paper with children in Florida's K-12 public schools.

Get them out now before you ruin their life.

---

[72] Ian Slatter, *New Nationwide Study Confirms Home-school Academic Achievement*, August 10, 2009 http://www.hslda.org/docs/news/200908100.asp

Education Reformation

While this may seem to be a bit harsh, let's look at the facts.

First, my best students every year are in order — Chinese, Eastern European, Indian and home-schooled Americans, and it is not even close when comparing this group to American public-school kids. Since it is highly unlikely that any of you plan to move to Beijing, Warsaw or Bangalore, you might want to look at the facts concerning public vs. home-schooled American students...

The home-schooled kids who show up in my classes usually arrive at the age of 16 or 17, score in the high 90's on their exams and then go off to places like Harvard, Penn and other world-class universities."[73]

As you can see, the home-school academic advantage has been verified not only by many studies from a wide variety of sources, but also by professionals in the field of higher education. Ultimately, Christians should choose to home-school for the glory of God as a way of fulfilling the Great Commission in their very homes, not for improved academic achievement. We are called to home-school for Heaven not Harvard. But thankfully, as we home-school for Heaven, we will not be sacrificing in the area of academics. If you would like more information on this topic, please go to the Home-School Legal Defense Association website: www. hslda.org

Question#3: Am I qualified to home-school?

Answer: Yes

There are many people who are insecure about teaching their own children. On a good note, the *Progress Report 2009: Home-school Academic Achievement and Demographics* study found that even home-schooled students from parents who had only the equivalent of a high school education scored 33 percentile points higher on their core scores compared to their public school counterparts.[74] As my wife likes to say, "You only have to be one page ahead of your child to succeed."

In addition, there are many home-school curriculums, including in depth daily lesson plans, courses taught by teachers using DVD's and/or the internet as well as Christian home-school co-ops that could help you succeed in teaching subject areas where you feel you are weak.

---

[74]Ian Slatter, *New Nationwide Study Confirms Home-School Academic Achievement,* August 10, 2009
http://www.hslda.org/docs/news/200908100.asp

Question# 4: What about single parent households?

Answer: The church needs to help the "widows and orphans."

> *"Religion that is pure and undefiled before God, the Father, is this: to visit orphans and widows in their affliction, and to keep oneself unstained from the world."* *(James 1: 27)*

In the world that we live in, providing a Biblical education through home-schooling is a challenging task even for families with a full complement of parents, let alone for single parent households. Since most single parent households are made up of single mothers and their children, I will be specifically addressing their situation in this section. Single fathers, take heart. Some of the same solutions can be directly applied to you as well.

For most single mothers, finding the time, energy, and childcare necessary to home-school their children seems like an impossible task. But it is not impossible, **"For all things are possible with God." (Mark 10: 27b)**. God has given single mothers countless mothers, sisters, brothers, and fathers in the body of Christ (Mark 10: 29 – 30) in order to help them accomplish the essential task of providing a Biblical education for their children. There are many ways in which the body of Christ could help a single mother home-school her children until she remarries:

Option#1: The church could financially support a single mother in order to enable her to home-school her children until she remarries or is able to establish her own home-based business.

Option#2: The single mother could move in with a Christian family from her local church in order to home-school her own children. This option would have two families come together as one household under the authority and protection of a single head. Having a single mother with her children join your household can be challenging in many ways, but if all of the household rules, procedures, expectations, and responsibilities are established and agreed upon before the single mother moves in, and they are all followed throughout their stay, this option can be a huge blessing for all involved.

Option#3: Many churches already have organized home-school co-ops where home-schooling families share in the responsibilities of content instruction and childcare. It would only take a few adjustments and added commitments in order to organize a stable rotation of single parents and volunteers from other homes-schooling families in order to provide the necessary childcare and content instruction support that single parents need.

Option#4: If none of the previous options are available, depending on the laws of your particular state of residence, a homeschooling family might be able to home-school the children of a single mother in addition to their own. I would only encourage this option as a temporary measure until one of the other three options can be arranged or until the single mother could start a small business where she could either work from home or take her children with her. Ultimately, the goal should be to have the single mother be heavily involved in home-schooling her own children.

There are so many different ways this could be worked out! Homeschooling requires flexibility. God will provide a way for us to do His will. Trust in Him!

ABOUT THE AUTHOR

Ray Fournier is a faithful husband who strives to love his wife as Christ loved the church (Ephesians 5: 25 – 33), and a loving father dedicated to raise his children in the discipline and instruction of the Lord (Ephesians 6: 4). In addition, he is a local evangelist and a public school missionary. He strives to live his life for the glory of God, centered on the gospel, focused on the Great Commission, and committed to the inerrancy, authority, and sufficiency of Scripture.

His commitment to live by God's Word as well as his 13 years of experience teaching in a public high school has led him to provide a Biblical education for his own children as well as to write *Education Reformation*. Ray's desire is to see our children saved and taught everything that Jesus has commanded (Matthew 28: 18 – 20), to see Christian families strengthened, the church experience revival, and to see our Lord Jesus Christ receive the honor and glory that He deserves.

Ray Fournier

Education Reformation

Made in the USA
Charleston, SC
12 July 2013